C0-AOE-500

Compliments of —
Author Burton

Leon Salzma

THE PATIENT AND THE THERAPIST

New Light on the Psychotherapist

Other Books by the Same Author:

OPERATIONAL THEORIES OF PERSONALITY
SCHIZOPHRENIA AS A LIFE STYLE
INTERPERSONAL PSYCHOTHERAPY
MODERN HUMANISTIC PSYCHOTHERAPY
ENCOUNTER
TWELVE THERAPISTS
PSYCHOTHERAPY OF THE PSYCHOSES
CASE STUDIES IN COUNSELING AND PSYCHOTHERAPY
MODERN PSYCHOTHERAPEUTIC PRACTICE
CLINICAL STUDIES OF PERSONALITY
CASE HISTORIES IN CLINICAL AND ABNORMAL PSYCHOLOGY

The Patient and the Therapist

New Light on the Psychotherapist

By

ARTHUR BURTON

HAMILTON PSYCHE PRESS
8330 La Riviera Drive
Sacramento, Calif.

THE PATIENT AND THE THERAPIST
Copyright © 1975 by ARTHUR BURTON

All rights reserved. No part of this book may be reproduced in any form, except for brief quotation in a review, without written permission from the publishers. Address inquiries to: HAMILTON PSYCHE PRESS, 8330 La Riviera Drive, Sacramento, Cal. 95826.

Library of Congress Catalog Number 75-22870

PRINTED IN THE UNITED STATES OF AMERICA BY
Theo. Gaus' Sons, Inc., BROOKLYN, N. Y.

For

EDITH HAMILTON BURTON

TABLE OF CONTENTS

Chapter   Page

Preface   xi

I   INTRODUCTION   3

PART I

PRIMARILY ON THE THERAPIST

II   LIFE STYLES AND THERAPEUTIC STYLES   9

III   THE WAY MEN BECOME THERAPISTS   28

IV   THERAPIST SATISFACTION   40

V   THE DIRECTIVE AND NON-DIRECTIVE THERAPIST   51

VI   ADORATION OF THE PATIENT AND ITS
       DISILLUSIONMENT   59

VII   THE THERAPIST AS PATIENT   78

PART II
PRIMARILY ON THE PATIENT

VIII THE FULLY-ANALYZED PATIENT 97

IX THE INTERMINABLE PATIENT 113

X THE PRESENTATION OF THE THERAPEUTIC FACE 125

XI HOPE AND PSYCHOTHERAPY 134

XII THE THERAPY OF A NON-DISEASED PERSON 144

XIII CONCLUSIONS 167

Index 171

PREFACE

MOST BOOKS ON COUNSELING and psychotherapy relatively ignore the ego and personality of the therapist. There is silent agreement that his mystique and work are best served by reducing his human aspects, and therefore his possible weaknesses. Therapists everywhere are by virtue of selection, training, and indoctrination more or less considered a unity and by virtue of this, interchangeable with each other. Nothing, of course, can be further from the truth.

Recent research on psychotherapy has repeatedly demonstrated the surprising finding that the personality of the therapist seems to be more important than his technique, and we therefore need to know more about such personalities. What are the lifestyles, values, interests, preoccupations, and attitudes of therapists? What kind of persons are they? Where do they come from? What makes them personally effective therapists?

This book, a collection of systematized essays, arose as a response to precisely this need. In it we take up many aspects of the lives of therapists not usually discussed in the literature. Some of these topics are the satisfactions of the therapist, the relationship of his lifestyle to his healing style, his dynamic childhood antecedents, the interminable patient, counter-transferences which bedevil him, the role of his face in treatment, the therapist himself as a patient, and similar others. In all of this the patient comes in for his share of discussion as well.

Our intent in this book is to focus on the humanness and genuineness of the healer as opposed to his screen, reflective, and cognitive purpose. Growth and healing take place through the fine nuances of the therapeutic interaction and it is these nuances that we attempt to describe in this book. This seems to us the true humanistic dimension in psychotherapy.

ARTHUR BURTON

Sacramento, California
May 1, 1975

Part I

PRIMARILY ON THE THERAPIST

CHAPTER I

Introduction

BEING A PSYCHOTHERAPIST is a desirable role in society today. There is evidence that this was true for the shaman (or his equivalent) in every culture of record; but it is even more so in Western culture. Being an analytic patient is also a sought-after role, for why otherwise should so many people become analyzed or treated. The turmoil of the final reaches of the 20th century with its loss of traditions and values, accompanied by the failure of the Calvinist work ethic, and a loss of personal meaning in life, makes counseling and psychotherapy more of a desiderata and value than ever before. Once again there is a pervasive need for a Mosaic figure to lead the children to the promised land of fulfillment. We look to Buddha, Lao-tse, Krisnamurti and other Eastern sages for guidance diminishing thereby Aristotle, Plato, Hegel, Freud, and Marx. Man with all of his glorious attainments and affluent state of being literally does not know to whom to turn to find his lost psyche or soul, and he has become suspicious of Western science and doubts that it can lead him anymore. Fifty percent of all men thus in desperation want to become healers; the remaining fifty percent want to become their patients. This is the way man seeks unconsciously to heal himself.

What is the meaning then of becoming a therapist in our time? What are its rewards and what its disabilities? What are the personal qualities which bring success to it? While we cannot yet answer such questions with any precision, the following comments may bear on the problem.

Being a therapist meets humanistic, power, intellective, emotional, economic and other needs. For the elect, it ties together conscious and unconscious dynamic needs which project themselves in unified fashion towards the growth of the patient. It has much to do with the therapist's own growth, and with the scientific concepts of growth and evolution which have guided science in the last century. It is also the sole situation in society in which one can be both the doctor and the patient and participate in both roles.

Psychotherapy is the basic dialogue of the Self and the Other and it is one of the most privileged interpersonal situations known to man. Nowhere are oral, anal, and phallic secrets revealed in such approved fashion as they are in psychotherapy. To be privy to the sexual person, to the intellections of the mind, to spiritual and emotional feelings, to creativity and its deficits, are all breathtaking in their human magnitude. Psychotherapy is not the "surgical" removal of a troublesome symptom—it is that too—but the most fundamental process of confrontation of the self with it-self, which mirrors thereby the great human encounters of history. Such an experience is not given to many, and the concealed hostility which accompanies it is easily understood. Where formerly the dedicated religious served in this way, they no longer can do so for many for one reason or another. Whatever it is, psychotherapy does help throw off obnoxious symptoms, and does reach the heart of the troubled person. The testimony of millions of patients, and the flourishing presence of thousands and thousands of healers, bear witness to its success.

Predicting the future is now a popular pastime, and also a social and economic necessity. Will psychotherapy/psychoanalysis vanish from the social scene? Will the coming biological engineering permit the selective breeding of people

4

without neurotic conflicts? Or at least will psychosurgery, brain implants, and drugs maintain people in simple tranquil control? Will the long, exhaustive effort required to look deeply into oneself—into the unconscious—no longer be required in the decades to come?

For us reflection, introspection, and thought are not about to be superseded by any new scientific development. Just as L.S.D. and psilocybine were first believed to be the *gran via* to creativity, self-awareness, and the unconscious, a kind of instant analysis to depths heretofore unknown, upon later experience they turned out to be only another way of evading the issue of reality and the ego. There are no shortcuts to writing a great novel or to living a great life. They both take analysis and synthesis in a most painfully penetrating way. Character and personality are fixed quite early in infancy and childhood and very few people are successful in ever changing them to a momentous degree. The vast majority are not even aware that their human situation may require alteration, or that it can even be done. The greatest ego resistance of all is the resistance to one's own growth and development. There will always be a psyche, a Muse, a soul, and men will ever strive for the highest levels of integration and expression possible for them. The more science provides them with leisure and longevity, the more will this need be evident. Total freedom from dis-ease brings problems of yet another psychological sort, and Pavlov's conditioning can reduce conflict and symptom but it cannot offer much on the philosophically positive side of life. Boredom, apathy, autism, and loss of personal meaning all increase in people as civilizations become older and when entropy does its work more efficiently. As this takes place psychotherapy will be more rather than less required by people. Its future is bright.

After a lifetime of study Rogers[1] formulates the qualities of the counselor which dynamically facilitate him in aiding the client as *genuineness, empathy, prizing the patient,* and the patient's perception of just these qualities. With this we

---

[1] Rogers, C. R. and J. K. Wood. "Client-Centered Theory: Carl R. Rogers," in Burton, A. (ed). *Operational Theories of Personality.* New York: Brunner/Mazel, 1974.

5

concur. However, they seem to us insufficient in and of themselves, lacking in a depthful parameter, and we would add the following to Roger's list.

1. *Experiencing.* The successful therapist is one who values and lives by his experience. Interpersonal contact, activity, ideas, and projects are his mode. He not only works but experiences. The mind is for him a growing, creating edge, and he is everlastingly urging it forward in his projects. Stasis, regression, deterioration, death, are all antithetical to him and he fights continuously to prevent their ravages in his patients and in himself. He is the visible demonstration that to experience is to be alive—to have and to fulfill a project is a step towards transcendence, to be followed by more projects and more transcendence. By his deep immersion in life, he testifies to the value and meaning of all life. Autism, fantasy, and passivity become the major indices of maladjustment for him and the demon to be fought.

2. *Artistry.* Psychotherapy is acknowledged as having as much artistry in it as science. In this one might say that the human interaction which is the psychotherapy involves more of behavior expression, language, and emotion than it does stimulus response in a chain reaction. What counts with the patient is not the objectively assessed situation of his life but how he perceives and responds to it. Much time, pain, and expense in treatment could be saved if one could go directly to the heart of a neurotic or psychotic problem. Some therapists think we can but this remains to be proven. The artistry of psychotherapy is imagination, play, humor, coupled to intellectual constructions, and set in an interpersonal framework. The artistic improvisations and syntheses of the psychotherapist is the same as with any artist.

The artistic components of the therapist's personality balance the cognitive/intellective in his makeup and in this way rationality can be coupled to emotion in a way which ends up in a well designed and pleasing therapeutic production. Without it, psychotherapy is apt to be heavyhanded, pedantic, and regressively classical. It does succeed, in its major endeavors, but it misses the finer points and the leaven

6

of existence. While the patient invariably rises up to meet the intellectual demands of the therapist, the patient must in turn descend into the depth of the unconscious to tap the therapist's emotional life. If therapy is kept only on the first plane, both participants sooner or later come to feel cheated.

As we discuss in a later chapter, there is such a thing as too much artistry in psychotherapy and not enough science. Such a healer comes sooner or later to be labeled a "wild therapist," signifying by the description that he has poor control of his improvisations. For us the therapeutic error is most often on the conservative side, with insufficient creation. Too many therapists have been taught to fear their unreconstructed artistic side, avoid it, and miss a certain dimension in psychotherapy. For this reason the Jungian idea of using creative modes of painting, sculpting and similar artistic forms as a part of treatment is a good one.

3. *Intellection.* There is no gainsaying the fact that psychotherapy is a cognitive/thinking activity in which the mind works at re-ordering and re-constructing things. It does this through the use of images, symbols, metaphors, icons, and the like and these are the tools of cognition/thought. The participants in psychotherapy are those who are the most skilled in language and symbol usage, and who are capable of extremely rapid mental processes. While analytical treatment can and does operate with children, illiterates, and even morons, it does so with a considerable handicap.

The various schools of therapy weigh cognition and emotion in varying degrees. Some therapies appeal almost entirely to the reason and intellect and others just as much to the emotional side. But the truth is that all therapy contains components of both. Therapy represents a gigantic "bead game,"[2] in which the intellectual monads (mathematics, logic, etc.) are fitted together to make a grand life design. Intellect, which the evolved cortex makes possible, is what distinguishes man from lower species, and must not be diminished in the total task of psychotherapy.

---

[2] Hesse, H. *Magister Ludi.* New York: Frederick Unger, 1949.

4. *Demonic Compatibility.* Psychotherapy is a profession in which patients bring their "bad" side to be converted to a "good" or "better" side. Even though in an objective sense the "bad" may not be so bad, the patient feels exorbitant guilt about it and his behavior is inhibited. It therefore becomes a therapeutic problem if carried beyond certain limits. But much of the patient is indeed petty, meretricious, narcissistic, and perverse. This is his demonic side.

Psychotherapy comes down to a struggle in which two demonic structures interact and joust for the fate or salvation of the one who is the identified patient. If, however, the therapist is afraid of his demon, and holds him too tightly in check, or rather he is afraid of the patient's demon, then the therapeutic work will be impeded. A therapist must have what we call demonic compatibility, or a comfort and familiarity with his demon, and it is surprising how rare this is to be found. This is the prime purpose of a training analysis or personal psychotherapy and most supervisorial work is justified by it. The demonic forms themselves are legion and they must be met in therapy on their own ground and worked through. But their manifestation is often coded and may be passed over if a special alertness in the therapist is not present.

Many of these matters are discussed in the following chapters. The focus is particularly on the therapist, his person, and the part he plays in the psychotherapeutic relationship. A companion book of ours, now being published, focuses in a parallel way on the interaction between the therapist and the patient, so that together the two make an ample compendium of practice and should be helpful to counselors and therapists on all levels.[3]

---

[3] Burton, A. *Interpersonal Psychotherapy.* New York: Jason Aronson, 1975.

CHAPTER II

Life Styles and Therapeutic Styles

WHEN A CULTURE BECOMES DECADENT and appears headed for extinction, new creative forms arise as compensation for the coming dissolution and which, it should be noted, are not always apparent but merely grounded in the unconscious of the creator or in nature. Primary examples are the Vienna of Freud and Wittgenstein, and the profusion of new plant life reported at Hiroshima after the atomic bomb. Some analogy may exist between such compensative phenomena and the increasing profusion of therapeutic forms in Western society. Along with a plethora of verbalized and unverbalized hypotheses which purport to explain man's inner life comes the most variegated of therapeutic styles all of which lay claim to healing power.

Psychoanalysis and its therapeutic derivatives are now at their apogee in Western society, but they are also being attacked by a new-wave generation called "radical psychiatry," as well as by a boring from within by psychoanalysts themselves.[1] The great vogue of encounter groups, transactional

[1] Alan Wheelis, a practicing psychoanalyst, has this to say about psychoanalysis in his recent book: "Psychology cannot lead us out of this desert. Indeed, the well-analyzed, well-integrated, well-dressed man in the grey flannel suit, with his liberal or even radical views, his experimental life stye, is in the same miserable fix as are we all, smoother perhaps but just as confused and heartsick." Cf., *The Moralist*. New York: Basic Books, 1973. P. 41.

9

analysis, primal scream therapy, and the like, are cases in point of radical subversion. These modes of treatment attempt to pump life into a psychiatric supposedly dead horse no longer seen as personally and socially viable or useful.

The goal of this chapter is to examine more closely the part the personal life style of the healer plays in his manifested therapeutic style and its meaning for the cure. The first implicit deviation in any socially controlled system of healing seems to be a subtle alteration in the mode by which the healer delivers his cure. Mesmer fell into organized medical disfavor not so much because of the substantive nature of the hypnotic phenomena he had by chance fallen upon as by the unique and charismatic nature in which he delivered hypnotism as treatment. Freud was always concerned about stylistic defections from psychoanalysis and monitored such deviations carefully. He was well aware that stylistic defections lead quickly to conceptual ones, and to a falling away from the psychoanalytic faith. Selection committees of psychoanalytic institutes are especially on the alert for embryonic heretics of this sort. Of course, we are talking here about the problem of the "wild analyst" and of the nature of "therapeutic wildness" itself.

It was Alfred Adler who demonstrated that a person organizes his life around his social needs and interests, and that these come eventually to be fixed into a kind of personality pattern which could be called a life-style. Adler's son, Kurt, has this to say about life-styles.

> The style of life, while influencing all its component parts, is not simply the sum of its parts, but generates its own unique quality in the course of its development. It also has a self-checking, built-in safeguard, precisely because any manifestation inconsistent with it must be rejected, or rechecked for its validity, or the assessment of the life-style must be revised by the therapist. This concept is the most definitive statement thus far in the field of ego psychology for the understanding and treatment of human character and behavior in all their seeming contradiction.[2]

---

[2]Adler, K. A. Life style in schizophrenia. *J. Indiv. Psychol.*, 1958, *14*, 68-72.

Adler, *pere*, began the life-style formulation with the concept of a "central purpose" in life and found that the neurotic either lacks such purpose or finds it overly constricting for his needs. In addition the neurotic defines his life-purpose more narrowly, more rigidly, and more fictionally than other people. From "central purpose" Adler derived "social interest," then "social organization," and finally came to "life-style" as the final summation of his ideas.

The term life-style has now become a part of the public domain as well as remaining a concept in the social and behavioral sciences. But it still serves a scientific need in that better than any other single concept it demonstrates how the personality constructs itself, and how it does so around some central organizational motif. Such motif the existentialists call the *reason for being*. Neurotics seem to have a startling defect in this form of organization and it gives them the special quality of perpetual search. They cling to their circumscribed and unevolved life styles as though they were imprinted to them, and to change them would be for them the equivalent of death. It is a legitimate research task to study comparative life-styles, and the values which derive from them, not only between the clinically neurotic and the normative, but among people, for example, who select differing vocational ways of spending their lives.

The therapeutic life-style has been described by a number of people,[3] and we have attempted this as well through autobiography.[4] In a capsulated way we might say that the therapeutic life-style is centered about the experience of suffering— and the alleviation of that suffering. To sit all day—and every working day—and listen to the complaints of neurotics is manifestly not to play football for the Los Angeles Rams or to be a Vice-President of the Bank of America. It not only involves a regularized passivity, but a curious selection of people to be with for almost a majority of one's life.

There is for the therapist no riddle like the riddle of the

---

[3] See, for example, Henry, W. E., et al. *The Fifth Profession*. San Francisco: Jossey-Bass Publ. Co., 1971.

[4] Burton, A. and Associates. *Twelve Therapists*. San Francisco: Jossey-Bass Publ. Co., 1972.

ego, and particularly if it has developed a malformation. Most therapists we know are not happy working in the vineyard of the normative; and those who venture beyond the garden-variety of psychotherapy and treat schizophrenics have the rare opportunity of "being present at the birthplace of creativity." In a later chapter, we will demonstrate that therapists become sensitized to emotional suffering and to problem solving by their own problem family structure in which holistic solutions to childhood problems were never really found.[5] This left them with an unconscious residue, or charge-mission, to solve *all* persons' family problems. They were thus ordained to become official or unofficial therapists.

Therapists as well are rationalists who prize the intellections of the mind. Images, percepts, symbols and metaphors are the magic of their healing transformations and, interestingly enough, these alchemically turn to gold. Therapists tend to be Jewish in origin in the greater majority, or are Christians who have unconscious Judaic counterparts; but they closely follow Freud in a kind of religious indifference or even hostility while still preserving their religious identification. And their daily work involves morals, ethics, love, hate, brotherhood, and matters of the soul. By personality they are on the solitary side, a feeling-intuitive-introvert, Jung would have typed them, usually demeaning and chafing their body, but within an aura of sensualism and pleasure. As a class they have an overweaning sense of justice and charity, and can be counted among the major humanists of mankind. They are fascinated by the demonic unconscious, even by the possibilities of psychosis, and, like C. G. Jung and Ronald Laing, turn their often unconscious misfortunes to good account. Such therapists struggle regularly with Eros (and Eris) in their patients, defer Thanatos temporarily for them, and extoll life and existence as a model in a number of ways. As a group they are anti-system, while yet serving in (and profiting from) one of the great organized systems of society.

A life-style differs from character structure in that it is

---

[5]A study by Mosak and Kopp of the early recollections of Freud, Jung, and Adler tends to corroborate this point. See *J. of Indiv. Psychol.*, 1973, *29*, 157-166.

more ego, more positivistic in thrust, and has more of a conscious philosophy behind it. A character structure is by and large lodged in the unconscious and is the final product of an entire series of dynamic developmental masteries or failures. It is far less subject to revision than a life style. The style of life is interpersonal, goal-seeking, and consciously directed toward achieving certain social and personal aims. White-collar and blue-collar stereotypes in industry have come to represent styles of life in which the latter "dirties his hands" and the former does not. In society the hipster affects long hair, an unwashed self, and an ambi-masculine-feminine exterior to demonstrate his disaffiliation with the corporate style of life. There is "funky chic," the "man in the grey flannel suit," the "village artist," and hundreds other life-styles which denote the self, its environs, and its strivings as it actualizes itself.

The concepts of self and ego are similarly not identical with life-style. Both these personality formulations, whether according to Freud or Jung or Rogers, represent organizational and executive functions of the personality, a way of differentiating self from other, and while they reflect a kind of stability of being, purpose, and behavior, they lack the ontic and social clustering-power of the style of life. There are people in the world who, for example, center their lives around feelings of depression (or joy), around their bodies, around special ideas, or other events. The ego mediates here against the id and superego in its quest but it does not make the election of the social interest or goal or drive it in its necessary direction. We might say that style of life is more teleological and character or ego more free of it.

The existential neurosis is more a function of life-style than of ego or self, in that the neurotic style of life, regardless of the nature of the conflict, makes no secondary gains possible for either the body or the mind, and, therefore, leaves a social vacuum behind it. The resident anxiety is not so much classically phobic as alienative, for anxiety of an unusual kind does appear when the pleasure quantum of the person—regardless of the nature of the conflict present—falls below a required level. Behavioral modification therapies rec-

13

ognize this point and force a change of life style by a variety of insistent stimulations and relaxations by which the patient begins to see that other styles are indeed open to him.

A recent book of ours even dares to claim the possibility that schizophrenia may be a life-style, a kind of devious social vocation, and not a disease at all. Schizoid maneuvers, autism, ambivalence, personality splitting, etc., are all slowly but insidiously learned, and become coded responses to family and social situations in which the victim so-called attempts a surrealistic approach to life rather than a real one. The classical forms of schizophrenia seem to be vanishing along with the state hospital which helped create them and are being replaced in society by ambulatory or pseudo-neurotic varieties, or what Lopez-Ibor[6] calls "schizophrenics at liberty."

Adopting the life style of a therapist requires a model from which a later disillusionment can operate as an almost inevitable event. Thus, it is usual for the therapist to begin as a Freudian, to perhaps later become a Jungian, or an Adlerian, or a Rogerian, or a Reichian, or a Rankian, and then eventually to become his own integrated man. He may more rarely be immediately ready for his own system, which he then propagates to others, but this is a matter of genius. Such modeling is an introjective thing, which not only requires following the master's theories and techniques, but incorporating life-style aspects of him. Freudians stand in the image of Freud and smack of him as a man. Jungians always have a little of C. G. Jung about them. Being a Jungian means not only subscribing to archetypes and the collective unconscious but more or less accepting Jung's outlook on being a person. The symbol of the Founding Father is not only the icon around which the principal thesis clusters but the mythic patterning upon which the therapist's life-style is erected. There is a feeling of security and certainty in it, as well as of being special or anointed in some way.

The life-style adaptations from the introject are always instructive. Freud loved solitude, contemplation, scholarship,

---

6 Burton, A., J. J. Lopez-Ibor, and W. Mendel. *Schizophrenia as a Life Style.* New York: Springer, 1974.

14

letter writing, extremely bright women, traveling, hostility to one's kind, and metapsychologic interpretation, among other things. These are now more or less the stigmata of the Freudian faithful. Eric Berne loved socializing, the comic, group approaches to healing, and quick analysis of ego behavior, among others. This is now the quality of the transactionalist. Carl Rogers is contained, honest, reinforcing, enthusiastic, and spiritual as a person. This for us represents Rogerians everywhere. Becoming a Freudian, a Jungian, a Rogerian, etc., is not so much an election as a need, and it brings social, intellectual and economic rewards as well.

It is therefore a serious matter to stop being a Freudian, Jungian, or Rogerian, etc., in midstream, for one has not only to give up Freud or Jung or Rogers but a way of life and its habitual appurtenances. Where we have seen this happen, or where a talented person has been denied admission to a training institute after the introject, the reaction is always an emotionally violent one, and more than rarely such a person may spend the rest of his lifetime demeaning what he has been denied, or competing with it—sometimes successfully.

The happiest of our clinical days are with the introject, and the demonic begins to enter when we seek to replace the Father, or at least to seriously abridge his gospel. This is the story of C. G. Jung, Adler, Rank, and others. Heretics have always received short shrift unless they have the genius and persistence of a Darwin, an Einstein, or a Freud. Every scientist interested in psychotherapy seeks a breakthrough in his field, a new understanding of the human condition, and ever more efficient ways of healing. At times such needs approach a compulsion, and the therapist may then, almost against his introjected model, and against rational processes, give in to his "wild" creative impulses in the face of his need. He unknowingly sets out to replace the master, first matching him stroke for stroke, and then attempting to outdo him. In doing this he gradually loses the built-in control of the introject and has difficulty discriminating the marginal from the legitimate—the complete person from the piecemeal one. We have always believed that there is this kind of strain in the systems of Jung, Adler, Rank, Reich, and others, where sur-

15

passing Freud was more important than the revised doctrine. Only in the letters of Pfister and Zweig, a theologian and man of letters, is this competitive factor really absent.

In physical medicine such problems are diminished for the physician has relatively short-term contact with the patient, is primarily interested in the patient's body, and the emotional aspects of the patient are relegated elsewhere. Indeed, those medical specialties which make room for greater emotional commerce with the patient reveal a higher suicide or addiction rate in the practitioner. Surgery, for example, where the patient's face is usually covered during the procedure, has a low rate of suicide among surgeons. These and similar examples reveal that the traditional aloofness of medicine toward the patient is no happenstance or shortcoming but a medical need which makes the practice of medicine possible to begin with.

We would therefore contend that psychiatry evolved as a modern specialty to make it possible for patients to talk to and be emotionally involved with their healers and to do so without disturbing the warp and woof of medicine proper. Transference is a safe and regulated way of emotional involvement with a healer. And the analysis of resistance is a distinctive method for titreing love and hate in proper dosages as a form of treatment. Medicine grudgingly tolerates psychiatry in this way because it well recognizes the necessary function it provides, and by virtue of it medicine can continue to organically "touch the body" without involving the personal feelings of the physician.

Every therapeutic style has as its fundament some life style. While training, professional identification, cognitions, etc., all contribute heavily to the evolved therapeutic style, we would claim that the life-style is most basic of all. Not only that, an evolved life-style seeks out therapeutic styles to be syntonic with it. One therapist extolls the rational in his system of healing and is impatient with the slow, classical, analytical development of insight. He urges his patients to rational understanding by clever and helpful cognitive tactics. But if one examines his own life-style, one sees that he is himself a highly rational person, lives by the many books he

16

produces, and takes instant and usually correct action on the many decisions in his life. He cannot do otherwise without falling into inanition or depression. Another therapist lived very close to his unconscious with its mysterious promptings, and was in constant communication with it. He valued its messages not only for the intercurrent data in his personal life but for its collective and universal meaning for all men. From this came a healing system based upon archetypes, symbols, and synchronicity without much attention to instinctual or childhood influence. Still another therapist sees man as perpetually good and attempts to bring out the best in him. The patient needs only the opportunity to clarify his "goodness" under a benevolent aegis, and to then use his experiences properly. And the therapist in this system must never be an interfering one but an everlastingly loving and understanding benign helper. Now, this therapist in personal life is a man of grace and goodwill, ever helpful, loving, and with a spiritual aura about him.

The examples of how the style of life shapes the practice of healing could go on indefinitely. Major theoretical constructions about psychotherapy or personality are more a matter of life-style than we would like to believe. Psychoanalysis is a product of the life-style of Sigmund Freud; analytical psychology is the life-style of C. G. Jung; and individual psychology according to the style of Alfred Adler. The healing paradigms are not so much scientific truths as experiential truths, backed by the inner needs of the creators, and held with a conviction upon which their very lives themselves are based. Such personal truths then become offered as universal ones. Certain novelists—say, Herman Hesse—were more open in this regard, for they acknowledged that the heroes of their novels were in their own cast. The battleground of sex (pleasure) in the last century of psychiatry, as an example, can be related to Freud's repression of it, Jung's incorporated acceptance of it, and Adler's indifference to it. Freud seemingly ignored Nietzsche, the greatest philosopher (of ideas) of his time; but Adler seized upon him for a theory of inferiority and power which he then generalized to all men because he presumably felt socially inferior himself.

17

Both Freud and Adler saw the phenomenon of social power in *fin de siècle* Vienna in different personal ways, and both ignored Wittgenstein, who had still another novel solution to offer man in his dilemma.

The therapists who do psychotherapy with chronic schizophrenic patients are a case in point. In an area which Freud himself enjoined candidates from entering, these therapists devote their time and energies to doing the impossible. They do not see it as a task but as a mission. To tackle the untackleable, to heal the unhealable, to succeed where others fail is grist for their personality mill. And to do psychotherapy with a schizophrenic patient is to put one's life at the disposal of the patient for, if nothing else, the binding parameters of temporality and spatiality do not count with them. While suffering is the root-attraction mode of all psychic healing, the quantum of it in the psychotherapy of chronic schizophrenia, and the mortification of the therapist which follows such attempt, cannot be so simply understood. It does, however, become more comprehensible, if we interpret it as a part of the life-style of the therapist—particularly the bedrock of that style. Just as certain physicists have to penetrate to the heart of the atom, some therapists have to perpetually discover the riddle of the schizophrenic "soul." Without this, they feel unrequited and a failure in their work.

Psychotherapy is an activity in which love, hate, and similar passions are the vehicles by which fixations are first clarified and then freed-up. Hillman[7] to the contrary, the power for change is vested in the emotional relationship between the participants, or what is formally known as transference. The abuse of that transferential power is known as countertransference. In no professional task is the self so much involved with the object of its ministrations as it is in psychotherapy. And this is both its hazard and its delight.

But it is precisely because the therapist can involve himself in this way with his patient, as compared to an engineer with a transistor, that the cure can go forward. The transfer-

---

[7] Hillman, J. "C. G. Jung: Archetypal Psychology," in A. Burton (ed.), *Operational Theories of Personality*. New York: Brunner/Mazel, 1974.

ence and "beyond transference" aspects of the psychotherapy are a Scylla and Charybdis ever present to destroy the therapist if he does not steer safely between them. A therapist is by definition a sensate person with a sensitive Muse and a desire to be involved. The wider and more encyclopedic his loving and hateful experience, the more mature he is. But his patient is usually a highly selected person as well and has latent capacities of a high order. More than infrequently patients are brighter, more talented, and have greater social or economic resources than their therapist. Where we excell is that we are masters of a sort of the unconscious, with its symbolic and archetypal forms, and the patient's intelligence often breaks down at this point and leaves him helpless to employ his powers.

Many therapeutic situations become temporary marital-situation equivalents (without sexual portfolio), and some may end up as life-long friendships. Some patients have been in therapy for two or three decades, and some gather a variety of therapists to themselves as experience. It is a way of life just as people today go endlessly from one encounter group to another. A few rare patients even marry their therapists; but a surprisingly large number do not last for more than a single interview and F. Scott Fitzgerald and Henry Luce are cases in point.

This merely illustrates a multi-fold opportunity to actualize one's life style through the healing of the patient. The patient may be acceptable to the therapist, or workable with, only if he is ego-syntonic in some way with the life-style of the therapist. The more successful a therapist becomes the more he discriminates from among those who apply and the fewer does he actually accept. His life-style has developed less capability of dealing with a failure. Aging as well in therapists brings with it a need to "tie up loose ends" in the lives of the therapists and it is a different experience than the first five years of practice. The covert hostility of the therapist toward his patients, and his practice, as a generic aspect of psychotherapy has never been fully acknowledged, and even Freud did not do his usual penetrating justice to this topic. The transference becomes at times a burden, and not every

19

patient can be loved and healed in the way he thinks he should be. There is a hidden therapeutic resentment for the patient being neurotic at all, for "laying it on" the therapist, and for the seeming ingratitude of successful patients who have left and vanished into the limbo. The "contract" with the patient for his treatment, and particularly the nature of the fee, is construed by many as aggressive and aggrandizing if not asocial. Therapy is more and more recognized as a power structure, and psychiatric power is becoming feared rather than loved.[8] While Szasz may be over-elaborating his point, psychiatry is an important institutional force in any society. Patients need us to be powerful, authoritarian, and have magic at "our command," but it is also because of this that they cannot get as close to us as they would like.

Carl Rogers, in summing up three decades of client-centered counseling, believes that what makes counseling effective are—to our interpretation—certain life-style aspects of the counselor. These are qualities of (1) non-possessive warmth, (2) genuineness, and (3) empathic understanding.[9] (We would add parenthetically that what makes a good patient are precisely the same qualities.) We tend, as stated above, to select patients who are syntonic with us, or who fit into our life style, and who produce their growth with a minimal necessary strain on us. Rogers has most of his life worked with receptive college youth and he found the schizophrenic patient difficult and disappointing in his first systematic assay with him.[10] Sigmund Freud treated a limited group of neurotics, and C. G. Jung liked the older and wiser patient. If patients we need do not come to us, we go to them.

---

[8] In California a law has just been passed limiting the use of ECT and psychosurgery to an approving consortium of psychiatrists for every treatment, so that the pragmatic effect is to ban these treatment forms. The resulting hue and cry has resulted in court action and a proposed revision of the law. The apparent stimulus for the law were patients themselves. Cf. Assembly Bill 1032, California State Legislature, March 4, 1975.

[9] Rogers, C. R., and J. K. Wood. "The Changing Theory of Client-Oriented Therapy," in A. Burton (ed.) Operational Theories of Personality. New York: Brunner/Mazel, 1974.

[10] Rogers, C. R. "My Personal Growth," in A. Burton and Associates. Twelve Therapists. San Francisco: Jossey-Bass Publ. Co., 1972.

This gives rise to the sometime observation that therapists who work in prisons have in their unconscious anti-social tendencies; those who work in mental hospitals are self-identified patients, and so it goes.

The critical question then becomes how much of an identification of therapist and patient, and the self-serving of life-style needs, is justified and curative. All of us are aware of how difficult it is to get an alcoholic or drug addict into sustained psychotherapy, unless of course the therapist is himself a former alcoholic or drug addict. Psychopaths respond most empathically to psychopaths, schizophrenics to healed schizophrenics, the obese to the formerly obese, and so it goes treatment wise. The principle here seems to involve a common (sometimes pathological) experiential pool from which peak and nadir experiences are drawn as sensitization factors for modeling purposes. But it is doubtful whether a list of sensitive traits, values, experiences, and the like can be drawn so as to hold generally for all therapists. The answer, as in Freud's time, still lies buried in the *dramatis personae* of the consulting room and what it is that brings such people regularly together. Rogers' criteria suffer from the over-simplification of a highly complex phenomenon.

We are thus logically led to the problem of the "wild analyst," the innovative healer who improvises beyond the capacity of the profession to receive his discoveries, or whose innovations may at times be a prelude to deviation or madness. An example, for the purpose of this book, is George Groddek.

Groddek was a peer of Sigmund Freud, almost a friend, and was highly successful as the operator of a private medical sanatorium. He had a restless, innovative mind, was a most capable physician, and saw more intensely than others at the time the relationship of mind to body. His local charisma can perhaps be likened to that of Charcot's. It has even been said that Groddek's "Book of the It" was the precursor of Freud's concept of the id, and there is evidence that Freud knew of it. Groddek understood the value of the new psychoanalysis, applied its principles to many of his cases, and even

21

went beyond it conceptually in some ways. Yet Groddek is unknown today.

The question thus arises as to why some "wild analysts" survive and go on to make extraordinary contributions and others equally gifted seem to disappear. Freud and Jung were also considered "wild creators" by their medical colleagues at the beginning and were shunned by the rank and file; but their contributions not only survive but occupy a central place in the accumulated knowledge of man.

The differences between Freud and Groddek seems to us to be in the nature of their ideas, and in the framework they provided for them. Kuhn says,

> . . . A new theory, however special its range of application, is seldom or never just an increment to what is already known. Its assimilation requires the reconstruction of prior theory and the re-evaluation of prior fact, an intrinsically revolutionary process that is seldom completed by a single man and never overnight.[11]

The truly generative man makes his discovery within a framework of needed knowledge, but contiguous with it. He furthermore dedicates his life to the further exploration and definition of his creation rather than immediately setting out to seek still another new idea. Groddek had brilliant ideas, executed them well, but they were not apparently related to the historical scientific past or future. They represented *ad hoc* creative explosions, which like roman candles fizzled out after trajectory. They lacked conceptual stability and historical continuity. Sometimes the generative stability of the imaginative process creating new ideas has to be called into question. Who can say at what point Wilhelm Reich crossed the line from brilliant scientific discovery to brilliant autistic surrealism, or worse? Every discovery of Freud's and Jung's had to find a proper place in a theoretical structure, or it was sooner or later abandoned. Where this was strained, for example, with the idea of synchronicity of Jung, and the

---

[11] Kuhn, T. S. *The Structure of Scientific Revolutions.* (2nd ed.) Chicago: Univ. of Chicago Press, 1970. P. 7.

22

death wish of Freud, they fell on relatively deaf ears and became so to speak extraterritorial. Innovative clinicians of this kind—say, nude or primal scream therapies—justify their imaginative techniques by the claim that "it works," and that patients approve of it. It becomes significant, however, that they make these claims in an area of therapeutic science in which no benchmark exists for the evaluation of the adequacy of treatment to begin with. It is precisely in psychotherapy that all theoretical claims must yet be honored equally whereas in a field of mathematics most of them would be immediately recognized as figments of beautiful imaginations. Modern society often rewards the "wild imagination" by economic return, and sometimes popular acclaim, but no such contribution can long outlive the death of the creator.

And yet, to limit creative imagination to the formalism of history and to current thought is to play into the cultural resistance to change. It is a sobering thought that Semmelweiss was hounded into a psychosis by a simple discovery that every physician today takes for granted as self-evident truth. Such examples in the history of science are many and there is no guarantee that they may not happen again. It may therefore be necessary to suffer every creation for awhile, and even the borderline mind, against the criterion of time and history and application. We are simply too imbedded in the treatment process as a value to yet be able to use scientific methodology to find what the truth is. Fools and geniuses have each been tolerated for this reason, and Don Quixote turns out today to be more a symbol of veneration than of laughter.

Where the therapist's life style has "wild" creative elements concealed in it, where he is forced to push the growing edge of the patient just beyond the point of convention, then the situation sometimes arises where charisma rather than applied historical knowledge cures. The personal power and meta manipulations of the therapist substitute for the medical or psychological corpus by which the approved cure is accomplished. In a field in which the personality of the healer is often considered more curative than his techniques, the situation is just ripe for charisma and mythology.

And there is a penalty to be paid which comes with what

23

at first appears to be a pioneering way of attacking a problem but is merely "wild." This is the process of personal disillusionment which follows ever faster and more frantic efforts to be even more innovative after a first public success. There follows a loss of respect for self and the acute sensibility of a lack of critical evaluation by others who count. The patient begins to be bored with that which first fascinated and helped him, and he moves on seeking more innovative and dramatic treatment, which was what brought him here to begin with. Finally, the healer begins to repeat himself, falls into a kind of irritable confusion, and then ultimately loses both disciples and patients. He often travels back and forth across the country delivering his "message," but it often ends in apathy, ignominy, or even death. Frederick Perls' vicissitudes come to mind.[12]

Extreme innovation or "wildness" by a therapist is a hidden dissatisfaction with his role. And yet he cannot abandon the field or look too deeply into himself. He rarely returns for further analysis. His relationships with his patients are meaningful and close, the economic rewards great, and he is in fact ill-prepared to do anything else occupationally on such a grand level. But as the years go on, the therapist internally diminishes, his life interests or life style changes, and he can no longer provide the concentration and tension necessary to his therapeutic work. He begins to take innovative shortcuts, wants success more quickly, and departs more and more from his introjected model.

A few write novels or non-fiction about the analytic situation, some escape into research or administration, but the majority—particularly if they are gifted—develop new theories and methodologies to meet their new life-style needs. This comes a great deal easier if one is not formally trained in a healing profession, as with some encounter group leaders, and who, therefore, feel they do not need to be guided by the healing paradigm of science.

When innovation becomes in a therapist a thing in itself,

---

[12]Perls, F. S. *In and Out of the Garbage Pail.* Lafayette: Real People Press, 1969.

it has appeared to us that intimacy pressed unusually hard upon such healer. That is, there was either a tremendous unconscious need to flee from therapeutic intimacy, or on the other hand to participate even more deeply in it. In the one, cognitive and rational paradigms are extolled; in the other, the transactional encounter of two bodies or two psyches are lauded. Every therapist is challenged by the erotic which his patient represents, and we use this challenge for the purposes of the cure. But since therapists are also men, and usually passionate or sensate men, a fine line separates the cure from personal experiencing. It takes years of learning, choice, and responsibility to consistently make such separation, and if the life-style carries unresolved erotic impulses, or the healer becomes subject to situational or ego-reorganization pressures, he may lose this balance and act out instead. The "art" of psychotherapy tends to submerge the "science" of it.

Psychotherapy is now in that social stage of creation or entropy where doubts and uncertainties call for a Messianic innovator (similar to Freud) who will "lead the children out of the therapeutic wilderness." It is like Freud's Vienna where the impending dissolution of the Austro-Hungarian Empire led to the most astonishing creative developments, including the birth of Zionism, linguistics, mental hygiene clinics, physics, architecture, music, and psychoanalysis.[13] The closing of the 20th century may have its analogues to the end of the 19th century in this way. For this and other reasons "wild" innovators should, in our opinion, be dealt with gently, for who is to say that a new Copernicus, Newton, Lavoisier, Darwin, or Freud is not among them? This is particularly true in a science as youthful as psychology. The invested paradigm of science over-protects itself from innovation and sometimes such protection knows no repressive bounds.[14] Culture has its own way of distinguishing the valid from the invalid, although it may be terribly slow about it. Freud never disintegrated under the trauma and desertions he suf-

---

13 Janik, A. and S. Toulmin. *Wittgenstein's Vienna.* New York: Simon and Schuster, 1973.
14Kuhn, T. S. *Op. cit.*

fered because he inwardly knew that his ideas had a numinescence which were based in a cultural revolution. He believed he was leading man to a more fruitful existence, a promised land, in face of the terrible burdens civilization imposed upon him. Similar to Freud, many men suffer the pain of scientific rejection, but nothing deters them from discovery. Are they perhaps historically selected in some way for their burden for the good of all mankind?

On the other hand, it is just as serious never to innovate. There are legions of men who never strayed from doctrine over a total lifetime. By and large, this serves society, for without a certain stability of "truth" and practice, professional anarchy would result. But psychoanalysis and psychoanalytic psychotherapy pride themselves on the fact that there is no analytic papacy, and no heretical inquisition. It gathers its principles and procedures to itself by reason, by social utility, and by cultural necessity. Anyone is free to leave psychoanalysis at any time.

It therefore comes as no great surprise that the life-style of the therapist is so closely related to the way he practices psychotherapy. And it is perhaps fortunate that such variations in style do exist. Out of them come not only a certain variety in healers for the patient to choose, and a subsequent matching up of patient and healer personal styles, but the creative evolution of psychic healing itself is made possible.

Of course, every professional science has the responsibility of limiting the "wildness" of its members. This is as well set down in common law. The primary medical injunction of "do no harm" is the most important of the healing covenants and millenia old. But within this, there are fairly wide limits in which small and large innovations and discoveries are possible, if not always immediately valid. These should be permitted access to formal communication media even though they do not sit well with editors and others in power. It is a sobering fact that Freud had to start his own publishing house to receive a hearing. Where the demonic, the sadistic, and the psychotic become recognizable features of the innovator, then the object of such impulses, i.e., the patient, requires protection. But even here, in the current pervasive-

26

ness of psychotherapy as healing, the dangers are presumably small compared to the social benefits of improvisation.

The real dangers of psychotherapy are to be found in a cool uninvolvement or disengagement by the therapist rather than over-engagement in the task. Too many therapists refuse to penetrate to the heart of the conflict; being content with symptom removal or substitution or placebo reassurance. There is an amotivational syndrome and a certain cynicism which may take over in psychotherapeutic practice over the years and its personal ravages can be serious. The "wild" innovator is usually immersed rather than ambivalent or nonchalant or hypocritical. Innovation is at least not as often guilty of "Goffman's professional staging of self." But, in closing, it must be said that the quality of the intervention remains one of clinical science's unsolved problems. Perhaps its most important one.

CHAPTER III

The Way Men Become Therapists

IT IS NOT EASY TO GENERALIZE about the way men become psychotherapists. In this chapter we have to be content for now with a sample of twelve outstanding autobiographies.[1] Even so, the twelve lives are less completely self depicted than one would like even though they were designed to be intensive. Having a psychoanalysis or a personal psychotherapy apparently returns less of the repressed to an autobiographer than we had formerly believed. Or possibly there is a greater reserve in professionals disclosing their childhood and development in this public way than we heretofore knew. Some reluctance to deal with the psychogenesis of their character was apparent in the twelve, and this reticence was paradoxically at odds with their often slavish interest in the infantile personality genesis of their patients. And, of course, female therapists have no part in our sampling, an obvious deficiency. Even though at the higher reaches of psychoanalysis

---

[1] The data upon which the formulations in this chapter are based come from twelve autobiographies written for me by outstanding psychotherapists—psychoanalysts, psychiatrists and psychologists—and published as *Twelve Therapists,* Jossey-Bass Publishing Co., San Francisco, 1972.

28

or psychoanalytic psychotherapeutic practice, and particularly in private practice, woman analysts and therapists are rare, two were invited to join this project, accepted the invitation, but were unable to deliver their manuscripts by publication date. Perhaps we can make a strength out of a weakness by confining our findings to the vast majority of therapists in our profession who are male.[2] Our twelve autobiographers thus do not at all represent therapists who are psychiatric social workers, educational counselors, marital counselors, and so on, among whom greater numbers of women therapists are to be found. But we would insist that psychotherapy *qua* psychotherapy has its own indigeneous requisites regardless of what sex practices it. Our twelve may indeed be more representative of a total social configuration than the small sample implies.

Seven of the twelve therapists are professedly Jewish. This ratio conforms well to the observation that this particular ethnic group applies for membership in healing societies in much greater numbers than their proportion in the population. Depending upon how psychoanalysis and psychotherapy are themselves defined, and how the sample is taken, Jews in the psychotherapeutic profession can range from a bare majority to an overwhelming one.

It may be that we have in these remarks overstressed the relationship between the dynamics of being a Jew and the dynamics of being a therapist. But the history of the Jews reveals that their particular social structure and needs led them to become healers in the Graeco-Roman, Arabic, Byzantine, Christian, and every other culture in which they lived. We might say that one does not have to be Jewish to be a psychotherapist, but it helps! We would also guess that those non-Jewish therapists who make psychotherapy their life style as well as their profession show an unconscious character similarity to their Jewish colleagues. Freud was always fearful that psychoanalysis might become a "Jewish science."

---

[2] We have earlier cited the fact that the fellowship membership of the American Psychoanalytic Association, the American Psychiatric Association, and the Division of Psychotherapy of the American Psychological Association is heavily male.

Perhaps it has—and now Jewish and non-Jewish practitioners merge into a single entity at the fundamental level of identification with the patient.

CHILDHOOD

Our autobiographers disagree about whether their childhood was determinative in becoming a psychotherapist. Albert Ellis flatly comes out against it; and Carl Rogers makes no great bones for such a possible early ordination. Werner Mendel, John Warkentin, and Arthur Burton, on the other hand, imply that their early character formation was causal in their becoming healers. And O. Spurgeon English seems to ride the fence. But what is assuredly manifest is that an early and sustained physical illness is almost uniformly found in the background of our twelve healers. English had tuberculosis; Ellis found himself with nephritis; Burton contracted bronchial asthma after flu; Rogers had periods of undefined lassitude; Warkentin had asthmatic attacks; Steinzor developed a disease of the eye; and so it went with all of them. These illnesses usually led to long periods of quietude and introspection, sometimes with an accompanying fear of death, and with a systematized fantasy which replaced reality as the source of childhood gratification. This fits well with the current understanding that "life flies in the face of one's disability." In some, handicap is followed by a superordinate attempt to overcome and compensate for it, along Adlerian lines, and the handicap becomes itself the sensitivity and justification for atypical dedication and effort. The handicapped try harder to make of this a nonhandicapping world. Bedrest, white sheets, nurses, physicians, medication, the total helping milieu, all slant the ego toward melioration. This strange supportive milieu then becomes the one of ease and comfort, and if a person cannot become a perpetual patient, one can at least become the doctor.

The family background in the twelve are remarkable in the absence of mental illness in the progenitors. One would have expected on an actuarial basis that the immediate or distant family would have had more psychosis in it. However, we would guess that psychosis drives people away from the therapeutic field whereas neurosis brings them to it. Psychosis overpowers and quiets the quest but neurosis activates the metaphorical search for the sources of humanity.

Our therapists come from families on the move. They were busy "making it," and particularly their fathers. Of course, not making it is also subject to the rule of being mobile. There is more than an average amount of it—intellectual, spatial, etc.—in these families and it is not to be accounted for by the European origins of many and their upward striving. As adults the therapists themselves show little stasis, and are galvanized people even though they exist in a relatively passive occupation. This high activity level partly accounts for the innovative creativity of our sample in the form of research projects, books, professorships, institute memberships, as well as substantial treatment loads. It also correlates with a certain volatility revealed by them as a group.

One would expect that as psychoanalysts or analytically-oriented psychotherapists, some of whom have been analyzed by descendants or even peers of Freud, these autobiographers would find early sexual trauma in their lives influencing them. But this book is remarkably free of sex and very strong on logos and spirit. Are these therapists saying that the primal scene, the evolvement of pregenital character, the castration conflict, the Oedipal conflict, and similar others were not important in their growth and development? Only Reuben Fine clings tenaciously to Freud's hard-won concepts and attempts—unsatisfactorily, we might add—to apply them to his own evolvement. As psychotherapists ourselves, we would say by way of explaining this phenomenon that such Freudian formulations are still very much there but serve as a baseline or normative aspect, and the authors feel that something more than a castration complex is needed to produce a psychotherapist and therefore pass it over. Clinical concepts anyway apply more readily to patients than they do to social producers and somehow fail to describe the fount of creativity. All of this points up the fact that the "sum of the erogenous zones" does not add up to what a person becomes, and the

31

self-description of a life is not indexed by its traumatic sexuality—early or late.

THERAPEUTIC TRAINING

Very few of our autobiographers have kind words to say about their training analysis, or their personal therapy in lieu, even though this is considered the focal point of becoming a therapist. Steinzor and Ellis are downright hostile; Burton, wistful; and Polster and English moderately worshipful and stargazing. But the "person" of the training analyst still shines brightly for them, perhaps in the understanding that the process was defective but the analyst tried hard and was quite human about it. All of them feel with great certitude that their true growth has come from, and with, their patients. Much of what they know they feel has been self-taught; that is, our healers have great capacity for an internalized innovative learning process and eschew or downgrade the formal learning methods available to others. In the face of this one wonders whether the requirement of a training analysis ought not to be reevaluated. We consider it extremely important, but largely in the sense that it allows the therapist to become an identified sufferer rather than serving merely as a learning technique.

THERAPISTS' WIVES

It seems necessary to be married to become an authentic therapist. The marriages of therapists seem to be very good or very bad, with not much in between. Our autobiographers reported that their wives have extraordinary meaning to them, almost it seemed to the point of sentimental embarrassment. Why is this?

At a workshop meeting of the Division of Psychotherapy of the American Psychological Association,[2] at which we were present, twenty-six therapists' wives met in an encounter group to work through their marriages to their therapist husbands. This unique group revealed that problems in their

---

[2] Phoenix (Arizona) Gazette, March 3, 1972. The group was facilitated by Dr. Ron Fox.

marriages are frequent and that they often feel lonely. Their husbands keep them and their patients carefully segregated and each therapist has in effect two "families" rather than one. But the wives were pretty firm in the belief that they also serve as "therapists" to their husbands—that they nurse them through Freudian, Rogerian, and other crises of evolution, and the many other pains which come from being a therapist as well. Many wives said they were jealous of their husbands' patients, and even of the joy they got out of their therapeutic dedication.

It is evident that our twelve autobiographers are in daily touch with their feminine side, are fundamentally related to —yes, in love with—women, and actually spend most of their waking (and sleeping) hours with women. The extraordinary number of female patients in society is certainly in part response to the welcome they receive from male therapists. But English's point is well taken: we treat female patients, but we marry our wives who are not patients. Our marriages endure beyond our treatment relationships; and they are, by and large, the more fulfilled side of us.

LOVE AND WORK

Each autobiographer talks of his love and his work. Freud was not far off in his description of them as the basis of mental health. And our therapists do work hard and love hard. In fact, the distinctions between love and work are often indistinguishable for them. The well-being of the therapist lies in the differential fact that he can love and work whereas his patient cannot. Being helped by therapy involves being able to work better, and to love more, that is to say, becoming more like the therapist. This is perhaps one of the reasons so many patients want to become therapists while they are in the process of being treated.

Management studies reveal that most people hate the work they do; but most healers find transcendence in theirs. And work and love are inseparable. Those who work unhappily tend to love unhappily. All true creative work has this power of disestablishing time and space; and joy, in the final analysis, is the momentary freedom from temporality and the idea of death.

LUCK

A surprising finding was the fact that our therapists believe they were the fortunate recipients of a process called *luck*. This is best exemplified by Rogers who calls it luck that he consistently anticipated and preceded clinical developments which put him on the crest of every tide in his profession for three decades. English and Polster and Warkentin and Ellis similarly feel this way, without explicitly calling it luck, and most of the other authors genuflect in this direction.

Is it that we feel lucky that we are not the patients? Do we consider the profession of psychoanalysis and psychotherapy so full of demonic pitfalls that luck has to rescue us, or is luck the symbolic statement of guilt about the good thing all of us have made of the misery of our suffering patients? Except in one sense we personally do not feel that we were lucky. We made our own breaks and consistently refused to accept failure. Some colleagues did accept it with less reason and fell by the wayside. Yes, we are lucky to be alive; but even here it is more a matter of genetic programming than anything the environment affords.

Ellis and Rogers best demonstrate careers in which, to us, luck played only a minor part. Each of these men had a finely attuned "third ear" which acted in radar fashion to bring them in harmony with the needs of society. They bet on themselves, and they bet on the receptivity of the environment to their presentations. But if the bet failed to pay off, they quickly switched to a better area of probability. Sex and encounter groups, rationality and self-help, are in wide demand, and Ellis and Rogers became specialists in each at just the right moment. Permanent failure is very rare in our group, and we doubt that it could occur. Only death can call finis to their enterprising being. If by luck one means a careful playing of the cognitive and emotive odds, then we have no objection to it. But creative men make their own luck, and modesty then leads them to ascribe their wonderful fruition to this evanescent lady.

BEING CRAZY OR UNIQUE

Our autobiographers accept the fact—even parade it—that they are unlike other men. This is a necessary part of their charisma; but this differentness is not only ascribed to them by others, it is a part of their own internalized image of themselves. To be "creatively crazy" is to be inventive and innovative—to be in touch with the devil, the unconscious, from whence all things stem. No therapist wants to be called a saint for this demeans the possibilities of his demonic and creative side.

As one reads the twelve autobiographies, it is surprising what illogical and irrational people therapists can be. Like Freud himself, who was an ass at times,[3] the child sits side by side with the adult, and is apparently as necessary to the adult as the adult is to the child. Thus Steinzor's six or seven years with his lady analyst makes us irritable that he didn't break it up earlier, for he desperately wanted to. And English tempting Thanatos while doing an internship with active tuberculosis, and Warkentin wanting to die because his wife spurned him, and Burton clinging to Los Angeles when the East called for his career is all straight *mischigas*.

These and similar behavioral examples are not the elegant and rational decisions one expects of mature therapists. Was it not the same with great writers? Dostoevski was a fool as a gambler; F. Scott Fitzgerald a sop about high society; Henry Miller carefully kept one step ahead of being physically heroic; and so it went. The successful Muse is a combination of cold intellectual steel and common drivel. Psychotherapy is a peculiar mixture of play and reality, of studied rationality and fantastic idiosyncrasy, of established maturity and puerile infancy, of sheer honesty and gross deception. All of this becomes critically focused in the personality of the healer, and the visible manifestation is often one of chaos. But we should not be fooled by this. In the crucible of the interpersonal relationship, which is therapy, all faculties zero in simultaneously and the therapist is there as razor sharp and authentic. He becomes for the hour almost perfectly integrated, as the

---

[3] See, for example, his letters to Fliess.

needs of the patient offer themselves to him, and he is effective. These autobiographers are sometimes funny as well as serious, and their comic aspect is just the recognition of life in its most serious and most comic aspects.

THE FUTURE OF BEING A THERAPIST

We suppose that the successful outcome of a life as a therapist is, as Mendel puts it, to move happily on to some non-healing joy. One simply cannot master all the seriatim challenges of therapy and maintain it on a constantly peaking level. The psychotherapeutic situation renews itself every day, but a more complex problem, or a more complex person, must always be waiting in the wings to support the challenge. Therapists find satiation difficult. To treat endlessly the same kind of people in the same way would be impossible for most of us. The many forms of current psychotherapies do not represent merely an artistry of process but the need to keep motivated in continuing therapy at all by a variety of innovated stimulations.

Countertransference is uniquely dissatisfaction by definition. Being a therapist requires working with the bedrock of existence and involves a perpetual philosophical questing. Irritability and dissatisfaction constantly wait at the door of the therapist to be let in. Psychotherapy is not a technique *qua* technique but the vocation of being human. To be human one must have human needs acknowledged and satisfied. We have for this reason called for an annual "satisfaction checkup" for therapists everywhere. Our autobiographers obviously do not reside in paradise, but they are a group of people greatly satisfied with themselves as human beings and have over the years fully actualized themselves. When they were not, they were quick to change.

SELECTION OF THERAPISTS

If one can to some extent generalize from a sampling of the lives of psychoanalysts and psychotherapists then one is left with the feeling that perhaps medical schools, graduate schools, psychoanalytic institutes, counseling centers are selecting the wrong people to train. The myths which abound about the selection of healers have a way of perpetuating themselves. The criterion of any selection quantum test for therapists must not only be a substantive number of ultimately recovered clients, but a sense of completeness and fulfillment in the doing of his job. The principal distinction we find in our twelve therapists from other therapists is not that they have helped great numbers of people but that they have become authentic and fulfilled people themselves by so doing. They like themselves as people and as therapists—a rare condition these days. But we are not so sure that all of them would be admitted to formal psychoanalytic or psychotherapeutic training programs were they to apply today.

If we may be permitted to use these twelve fulfilled lives as a criterion and assume that they stand as some kind of model for future generations of therapists, then the following would be among the relevant criteria for selecting candidates for healing work in counseling and psychotherapy. Their absence may not necessarily result in the failure of any candidate, but their presence is most definitely associated with his success.

(1) A therapist is a person with a metaphysical hunger.

(2) A therapist idealizes his father and often depreciates his mother.

(3) Love and negative mutuality will be central to the therapist's being.

(4) The therapist will feel comfortable with hearing "confession."

(5) The therapist will live closer to his unconscious—and thereby enhance his consciousness.

(6) The therapist will have personally experienced existential depression, despair, anxiety and similar life emotions.

(7) The therapist's family background will reveal considerable creative disruption and upheaval.

(8) The therapist will symbolically require not one but two marriages and families.

(9) The therapist will introject a therapist-ideal and will

---

4 Burton, A. *Interpersonal Psychotherapy. op. cit.*

find creative meaning in the yin and yang—the love and hostility—of such idealization.

(10) The therapist will be an intellectual and rationalist who interprets his world as orderly, logical, and subject to cognitive rule.

(11) The therapist will place a high value on talk and conversation as a means to insight and fulfillment.

(12) The therapist will manifest a deep logos but will not be institutionally religious.

(13) The therapist will be a liberal, social activist but will actualize this through his patient rather than through his behavior.

(14) The therapist will primally manifest (Heidegger's) Sorge. He will have a Promethean caring for humanity and a willingness to assume the absurdities and guilt of man.

It could be said that some of our twelve famous therapists have moved along with the times and others appear to still represent the more traditional beliefs of psychotherapy. But are we to value one group over the other? My feeling is that Carl Rogers is Carl Rogers is Carl Rogers whether he is being a client-centered counselor, more directive with schizophrenics, or a self-effacing facilitator in an encounter group; that it does not matter much which. The social forms by which a therapist plies his healing philosophy are almost irrelevant to his treatment outcomes. Every therapist in the early stages of his growth finds a platform from which he leaps into the "faith of the cure," and the fact that some leap further or more often than others is not in itself remarkable. What counts more highly is what we have described in the 14 points above, but more than this, the summation of all of them into what we call the primal healing posture of the personality. If such Sorge is present, then the healer can be expected to be motivated to heal, and to offer his ego time and again in the service of the disabled. Without it formalism is apt to take over, and the whole process defeats itself.

Training institutes are confused as to who makes a desirable candidate and whom to admit and not to admit for training. They oscillate in their admission policies as the social tides go. We want boldly to say that these twelve are for us the heroes of psychotherapy and future candidates for psychotherapy should be accepted principally in their image. This is not vanity—it is that too—but a lifetime demonstration by these healers of a clear and brilliant extension of humanism to the dehumanization of the mentally ill. Not only that. These twelve people have provided society with vast quantities of creative productions which have extended art and science beyond any expectation as to their numbers. In this they have more than carried their weight as social models. The failure of psychotherapy is precisely that so few clinicians go beyond the patient to the creative written word.

The psychotherapeutic process, in our opinion, has not yet reached its apogee, and in the desperate social need of our times, it is being widely secularized. But secularization and heterodoxy seem to be falling short, and again and again we find that we cannot escape the basic discoveries of Freud and Jung which renew themselves again and again. Process abridgement for comfort, convenience, and palatability has limits. Perhaps we have now reached them. A man a long time ago said to us: "There are no bargains or short cuts in psychotherapy; it is fruitless to look for them." We now fully agree.

CHAPTER IV

Therapist Satisfaction

FREUD NOTED MANY YEARS AGO that the psychoanalytic situation was one. that gave little satisfaction to either of its participants. It is commonly known that the patient products of a long-term psychotherapy, including a psychoanalysis as well, feel just as often unrequited in their long quest for fulfillment as they are pleased with their therapeutic outcome. For a process in which love and positive regard have such a central place, this finding is indeed a paradoxical one. Perhaps the feeling one has about the outcome of one's analysis is not necessarily correlated with the good it does. One at any rate seems to feel generally that a mother, father, doctor, or lover should have done more than has been done in any interpersonal transaction.

We make an attempt to please the patient, to make the therapeutic situation the least stressful for him, and we want if possible to have him go away happy at its conclusion. The fact that this occurs so infrequently is part and parcel of the whole cultural question of the value of psychotherapy itself. But my focus in this essay is something of a different order. It poses the question of the satisfactions of the psychotherapist, and what he seeks from his patient. My contention is that the satisfactions of the therapist are as equally important as his patients' and, even beyond this, they can make or break the treatment by their countertransference implications. There is almost a conspiracy in psychotherapy in the refusal to look at the satisfaction-needs which a psychotherapist has. This of course comes from medicine where healing has had a quasi-sacred function extending back at least to Aesculapius and Hippocrates. For this reason the economic aspects of medicine come as a great or small shock to patients who everlastingly expect their physicians to be modeled after Saint Francis. Observations of psychotherapists for three decades at national conventions, and knowing them intimately, reveal that they are indeed quite human, perhaps on the sensual side, and need constant reward-reinforcement as well. Their wives complain of their husband-therapists' need for mothering, and they are just like all people in their nurturing needs.

While we will detail a suggested scheme of therapists' satisfactions later, some preliminary comments may be in order here. The first has to do with fees; the other, the selection of patients we treat. The more one practices psychotherapy, the less important does the fee become as an interpersonal motive to heal. The principle of surfeit applies to fees from psychotherapy in the same way it does to any entrepreneurial earnings. In the presence of a waiting list of patients, the fee becomes a practicality rather than an issue, and most often takes second place to temporality as a vicissitude. The fee charges represent a host of social and personal variables, such as professional standing in the community, self-worth, the financial resources of patients who apply, the style of life of the therapist, greed, power needs, and the like. But once a level of fee income is attained which is syntonic with the therapist's conception of himself, the vicissitudes of the therapy itself has little or no correlation with the fee charged. It is interesting to read in this regard Freud's report of his anxiety, after founding psychoanalysis and expecting referrals, at how rarely they came, and the joy he felt when a patient actually did appear. The answer to the therapist satisfaction question cannot be found in money.

41

As we become more and more successful we become more and more discriminating of the patients we accept. There seems to be a "going beyond oneself" to find patients who challenge our growing edge and keep us deeply immersed in the therapeutic process. As it was with Freud, one looks for that special patient who will provide data for a scientific breakthrough, or who instead has special qualities of beauty, intelligence or artistry. From such patients we learn a great deal, or we receive a great deal of satisfaction, or both. This is indigenous to all learning or Socratic processes.

All psychotherapy calls for more or less intense relationships in which Eros catalyzes the movement toward growth and reduces the ever ready pull of Thanatos. To believe that Eros can ever be applied in healing with objectivity is wishful thinking. Medicine protects itself from Eros by white coats, extremely brief intervals with the patient, instrumentation, medication, nurses, prominent displays of photographs of wives (husbands), etc. But such devices are not readily open to all non-medical psychotherapists, who are anyway in the majority, even if they should be deemed helpful to psychotherapeutic goals. But Eros also makes it possible to exploit the patient, who too often plays into his own misuse. Freud realized this and went to extraordinary lengths to restrict socialization and fraternization between analysand and analyst. In part this was due to his own separateness, but also to the very real fact that the psychotherapist has to be something other than a friend, guide, or lover if psychotherapy is to heal. Even so, more than the public ever learns, physicians do make personal friends with their patients, socialize with them, and even use them in certain novel ways. It appears at any rate that the brief, medicative, instrumental, more or less objective model of medicine cannot be directly superimposed on psychotherapy insofar as the human transaction and its personal meaning is concerned.

Our biographical study of the lives of twelve outstanding therapists[1] revealed that they had not resolved their own family romances and that they furthermore felt unconsciously

---

[1] Burton, A., and Associates. *Twelve Therapists. op. cit.*

required to do so. They were unusually sensitized by this to the human condition, to emotional pain and suffering, to Eris and Eros, and were driven to relieving burdens in their patients and helping them to find joy. If such a background is prototypical for all therapists, it can be seen why the entire question of satisfaction for the therapist becomes uncomfortable. Where needs are met beyond the professional situation, guilt and shame are their accompaniment. But we would still insist in the face of this that only when the growing edge of the therapist is fostered and he receives satisfaction is his psychotherapy truly successful. It therefore becomes necessary to explore the ways in which this can be done rather than assuming that the therapist has no need for personal satisfaction in his work.

The satisfactions of the psychotherapist as a person can be dichotomized as those which take place *outside* of the therapeutic hour, and those *inside* of it. Taking the former first, what can we say about the extra-therapeutic activities, fulfillment and happiness of the therapist? It must at the outset be said that not much is known about what therapists do when they leave their offices. It is clear that most of their needs are met in family living, in cultural pursuits, in travel, and in small group gatherings of many kinds. They tend to have little interest in sports, finance, religion, politics, or gross molar activities, carrying into their recreation their focal interest in the symbol and psyche. They are not unlike Sigmund Freud or C. G. Jung in the joys they have outside the consulting room.

The problem arises when the outside satisfactions, for one or another reason, are just not there. There may be a bad marriage, overconcern with finances, considerable use of alcohol or marijuana, depression, somatizing, and the like. Where these are not quickly resolved, strain is placed upon patient relationships for satisfactions which should come from outside. Inhibiting countertransferences then come thick and fast.

The therapeutic situation is one of relative unfreedom for the therapist and makes restless therapists of us all. It is one reason violent confrontations occur from time to time in

43

therapy. The classical passivity is simply too difficult for some therapists to bear and so *active* forms of therapy—encounter groups, psychodrama, transactional analysis, etc.—have historically evolved. In my experience, dissatisfaction with being a therapist, or chronic or regular dissatisfaction with specific patients not only inhibit the forward-going motivation to cure which needs to be sustained for years, but deprives it of emotional content, those structures which are the foundation of insight and growth. There thus begins an increasing inner struggle to maintain self-motivation, as well as other-motivation, and the deceptive ego-devices, the cover, fall by the wayside one by one. The *post-hour depression* following a bad therapeutic hour is not a very pleasant thing and not too many such bad hours can be tolerated in any one course of treatment. When the therapist's own parapraxes begin revealing his difficulties to his patient, he is then in danger of "leaving the field." The satisfaction process is best illustrated in the psychotherapy of schizophrenia, where the field is strewn with defectors, and even a few corpses. The question then becomes: Do we ask our patients indirectly to make up for our unhappiness? The answer must be, for some therapeutic situations, "Yes."

It goes without saying that similar to any work situation the therapist does what he can to reduce the boring and satiating aspects of his work. This involves an office in which he is at home (and even loves) ; a selection of case material which challenges his own development; a temporal frequency of visits best suited to his temperament; interfaced activities and diversions which give relief to therapeutic stress and strain; and a variety of similar others. We ourselves find our best involvement and motivation with what we call "Harvard types." But these are actually patients of ours who have been to Harvard! We are less interested in the character disorders, and are grandly involved with the neuroses and psychoses. In this way we give ourselves the best opportunity for maximal involvement with those patients we do take on and can be involved with.

But this is only a part of the story. There are, as we see it, six variables of satisfaction arising from psychotherapy which we want now to discuss. Our findings are that if the therapist receives high ratings in at least four of them, he is a "satisfied" therapist. They are: (1) intrapsychic satisfactions; (2) sensual-interpersonal satisfactions; (3) intellectual-rational satisfactions; (4) research-creative satisfactions; (5) cultist-fraternal satisfactions; and (6) economic ones.

1. *Intrapsychic*

The joys of doing psychotherapy, the pull toward patients, has been variously described. But on both real and metaphoric levels it allows a kind of experiencing not open to people who are not therapists. On a real basis it gives the psychotherapist an "inside seat" at the widest panoply of human proclivity and behavior. In our own experience with patients we have been involved in the manufacture of guided missiles, lived in the world of surgical medicine, sat in on the jazz and concert scene, played the stock market, taken part in the political arena, watched the infighting in the political university backwaters, experienced the world of psychiatry, and an important number of others. Had we not been psychotherapists very few of these social arenas would have been available to us since we do not qualify by skill, social position, or in several similar respects. As one therapist puts it, "Such vicarious pleasures do much to help me accommodate to the lives I never can live."[2]

But this is not what we mean by intrapsychic satisfaction in psychotherapy. It is instead the awe of being present at the birthplace of an individual's creativity—of that psychic aspect of ontology where the ego is formed and extruded with our help. It is participating in that great mysterium of life, which if expressed, stands forth as the numinous symbol which reduces language and motor action to a stammer. To help a crippled ego exert its potential strength, to actualize itself, is to combine the Eros/Thanatos equation into a more workable life situation. The joy of seeing suffering turn into its exact opposite is the intrapsychic satisfaction discussed here.

[2] Steinzor, B. "The Mystery of Self and Other," in A. Burton and Assoc. *op. cit.*

Beyond this, is the understanding that one becomes a psychotherapist not by selecting a profession but by "being called" to it. Because of an incomplete early family romance, the idealization of the father and depreciation of the mother, the historical Jewish or crypto-Jewish affinity and identification, the love of rationalism, the incorporation of the psychiatric hero, the preoccupation with "talk" and the "word," and similar personal and social processes, an intrapsychic hunger is set up in certain personalities which finally results with time in becoming a healer. It is such unconscious needs rather than the more conscious ones which play themselves out against the interpersonal therapeutic setting with a feeling of growth, achievement and satisfaction and which is precisely that intrapsychic reward of being a psychotherapist.

2. *Sensual-Interpersonal*

Psychotherapy is a sensual business and it is no happenstance that the couch is its popular symbol. Psychotherapists are perhaps more sensual than other people, but they act out their sensuality less. Love and affection are the currency of this form of healing; the fact that vocationally one is everlastingly being titillated by Eros makes an assumption of needs of this sort necessary.

But sensuality is not sexuality. One actualizes sexuality at home with a wife, but idealizes and fantasizes it with the patient. The latter rarely meet the wives, or become wives. If the "two families" should become confused in this way, then both treatment and marriage might suffer. But the fact that the overwhelming majority of psychotherapeutic patients are women, and the overwhelming majority of psychotherapists men, indicates a cultural heterosexual attraction. This sensuality is what gives tone to psychotherapy, and provides for a part of the special excitement connected with it found in few other professions.

3. *Intellectual-Rational*

Talking is a central avocation of many ethnic groups, and even favored by some over gastronomy. In the Jewish person—the predominant ethnic representative among psychotherapists—life could hardly go on without talk. The "people of the book" are the people of the "word"—and by extension, the symbol. The verbal image supersedes the organic image as the vehicle of communication, which is perhaps why the body more than often rebels in this group. The dialogue makes silence a painful thing, even an enemy, for the social goal is face to face *talk*, mirroring ultimately, we suppose, Moses on Mount Sinai. Talk is as well the "written" word, for some talk better by writing, and a book represents clarified and stylized talk honed to a fine point. Therapists do write many books.

Morons, as we have said, make poor patients, because they have so little to talk about; but also because they lack that royal symbolic vehicle for transporting mental content. That is, we rapidly become disinterested in treating morons for they seldom have anything to say to us and they lack the symbolic orientation. People of intellect are, however, another matter. Is it because the middle-class parameters from which we spring are the same with them or because their rational-intellectual world outlook is otherwise syntonic or because the social structure of the neurosis applies equally to both, that we are more comfortable with their intellect and their self? Whatever the explanation, the intellect ranks supreme in psychotherapy, and talk and symbolic interchange with people who "belong" closes the gestalt of pleasure and allows both to thereby go forward. A Ford Motor Company assembly line would for a psychotherapist be a Sisyphusean fate.

4. *Research-Creative*

Psychotherapy is not commonly thought of as research, and yet in the hands of Sigmund Freud it changed an entire culture as a method of inquiry. Research *qua* research must have social effects to be useful and, in this sense, research which takes place in clinical or healing settings qualifies. It is impossible to do psychotherapy for extended periods without that special need to inquire and understand which is the fundamental basis of scientific research. Yet, it is also true that relatively fewer clinicians set down their findings in comparison with other investigators, and Freud was a rare bird in this way.

An important satisfaction in doing psychotherapy is that one closes the circle from hypothesis to fact. That is to say, that the hypothesis of the moment, the hypothesis of the hour, of the total number of hours, is tested against a set of operations, and then lead to negative or positive generalizations which are the growth alterations the patient makes in his world. The fact that a suicide or a homicide often rides on the outcome of a psychotherapy makes this the must crucial of all research. And this is one experiment which cannot be replicated! All psychotherapists have the oceanic feeling of being involved in a momentous life research, along with doing treatment, and, should this feeling be missing for one reason or another, their psychotherapy and they themselves lose a dimension.

Creativity is psychotherapy. A patient is by definition a person who is non-creative but needs to be more creative. Psychotherapy is a shared creation, and to offer it, the therapist has to have more creativity than his patient does. Such creative potential need not be formal scientific research method, and quite frequently it can involve the arts in their broadest panoply. The Jungian conception of the artistic and scientific in the psyche applies here in a useful way.

5. Cultist-Fraternal

Being a psychotherapist is a socially privileged position and makes one a member of a special fraternity. Large numbers of people want into this fraternity, and perhaps just as many set obstacles to their admission. Whether one formally belongs to a psychoanalytic institute or not, professional institutional grouping of some kind is the rule. Very few therapists can tolerate the loneliness of practice without buttressing it in some way by membership with their own kind. The fact of a generalized cultural hostility toward the therapeutic process and to therapists themselves results in a counter-identification (and arrogance) which further serves to throw therapists together.

Under stress not only the worst but the best offers itself. While our profession is not known for its "sweetness and light," it doesn't differ greatly from any important social area which counts in the scheme of things. But our feeling is that something very important is involved in therapy, and that no one else—certainly not the clergy, or the lawyer or the educator—can provide it. The psychotherapist feels himself the chosen one.

There is thus a special tension and satisfaction in the congregation of therapists in whatever form it takes. Indeed, the extra-therapeutic social life of therapists, as it does in medicine generally, shapes itself around the personnel of treatment and its literate, artistic, and social involvements. It is a satisfying cult.

6. Economic

We have deliberately placed the economic rewards of psychotherapy at the bottom of the pile without of course thereby minimizing them. The fees one earns in treatment work, or in a salary paid for doing the same, determine many important facets of our lives. If one prefers travel, country club membership, owning a sailboat, collecting rare books, etc., fees from therapy make this possible. Membership in a psychoanalytic society, or its equivalent, automatically brings with it an upper-middle class value system, and the means of satisfying such values.

But we all discover that the longer we practice therapy—the more we are successful at it—the less we are charmed by earning money. This is what we call the devaluation of the fee-reward. It applies as well to other professions. One may still seek money, but it will usually be found in writing a best seller, in the stock market, in real estate investments, etc., but not in doing more therapy itself. Increasing the number of difficult patients, or even the absolute number of patients treated, makes for more income, but the ability to use that income falls off even more rapidly. But it is certainly

49

gratifying, even a position of privilege, that psychotherapy pays so well, in addition to the other satisfactions it offers. Without this fact, and to be honest about it, the field might lose a portion of its glamor.

In summary, the message of this chapter is of course that the therapist had better look to his satisfactions. A fulfilled life outside of therapy is the desideratum. But even here, we would not want to relinquish the special beauty—and hazards—of the therapeutic situation. If we had wanted to, we would have stopped being therapists a long time ago.

CHAPTER V

The Directive and Non-Directive Therapist [1]

IN THE LAST SEVERAL YEARS there has been a decided movement towards therapies which are more direct, cognitive, instrumental and more rapid than heretofore manifest. This shift dynamically involves less of the relationship of the patient to the therapist, the Rogerian healing attitudes of positive regard, etc., and more of a direct intervention in severing the association between the unwanted behavioral act and its neurotic stimulus structure. The current examples of behavioral modification, bioenergetics, psychodrama, transactional analysis, hypnotherapy, primal scream therapy, and a host of others make the point. It is as though the non-directive approach has suddenly been found wanting and been superseded by its counterreaction. It is also notable that in a curious paradoxical way non-directive counseling led to the philosophy of the encounter group in which direct confrontation between self and other is the currency of growth. Some of the most violent therapeutic directivity we have ever seen

---

[1] Client-centered and therapist-centered terminology are a more up-to-date version of the directivity problem. We will cling to the classical usage in this chapter.

has occurred in marathons and other extreme forms of encounter groups. Farson, in summing up this situation, has this to say:

> But today's practitioners are impatient. They are not satisfied with such a pedestrian approach. They argue that if it is beneficial for people to talk about their feelings then perhaps it is good to make sure that they do. To accomplish this all sorts of gimmicks have been invented to elicit the expression of feelings. From there it was a small step to *force* a person to talk about feelings. If there were no feelings to talk about, ways could be found to make sure that there would be feelings to talk about. And if tears accompanying the experienced feelings gave them more validity, then screams or nausea would be even more valid. So it has gone, and in the process Rogers' idea of respect for the person is in danger of disappearing. Authoritarian gimmickery seems irresistibly satisfying, even to humanistic psychologists. Rogers himself is sometimes caught up in this trend. Performance seems to be winning out over safety, aggressiveness over acceptance, emotionality over dignity. The newest forms of treatment to which people are flocking by the thousands are almost neo-fascist in their willingness to use coercion and threat to evoke feelings which supposedly can then be explored to advantage.[2]

This chapter was written because it always seemed to us that the question of directive or non-directive therapy was one of sometime sophistry, established a false typology which had no real basis in reality, and served to indirectly stigmatize those psychoanalysts and therapists who were more assiduous in approaching their patients with varying techniques. And further, that casting the problem of therapeutic attitude in this light encouraged an inevitable counter reformation which provided a base for the development of directive techniques way beyond our previous experience. Our task in this chapter is to analyze some of the facets in this bit of history of psychotherapy.

---

2 Farson, R. Carl Rogers, Quiet Revolutionary. *Education*, 1974, *95*, 197-202.

We suppose that the directivity of a therapist can be measured by the number of interpretations he makes in a therapeutic unit of time. On this kind of scale, the early Rogerians would most certainly be at one end and John Rosen or Albert Ellis at the other. No one knew better what a total weapon interpretations could be if used incorrectly than Sigmund Freud. It is because he knew this that psychoanalysis is such a drawn out process, for he felt that the prologomenon or preparation for a supremely important interpretation required weeks, months or even years to attain. Revisionists found this preparatory period extremely chafing, sought quicker ways of achieving it, and finally lodged upon formal or informal group methods where interpretations were given immediately (safely it was thought) within the snug shelter of the group cohesion. Group facilitators never feel better than when a member of the group is distraught and crying with relief! And it did finally become clear that making an interpretation was not as individually dangerous as Freud had believed.

What of course had taken place in the spread of the non-directive philosophy was the denial of the unconscious. Non-directive counseling always acted as though a person were fully conscious and that behavioral change was simply a matter of will and clarification of emotion rather than a searching in the well within. In this, Rogers was influenced by Otto Rank and his will therapy. When Rank split with Freud and began denying old analytic precepts he sought relief from the long-term analytic process and abbreviated it in this fashion through the use of will.[3] There was always a kind of purity about non-directive counseling which made the worldly and experienced therapist blink in disbelief for he knew well of the demon inside of his patients. But non-directive therapy was made plausible when highly intelligent, superbly motivated college youth became the principal subjects of its healing aegis, but it later broke down badly with schizophrenics, corporate executives, depressives, and more involved patients generally. It was, we felt, a better technique

---

[3] Roazen, P. Freud and His Followers. New York: Alfred A. Knopf, 1975.

with the non-diseased than with the sick. Non-directive therapy, in its final formulations of genuineness, prizing the client, and empathy, came uncomfortably close to the message of Christian brotherhood which, if the truth be told, seems to be a philosophical and ethical failure in the modern world.

From the early and brilliant findings in various university counseling centers, it was hoped that the non-directive viewpoint could be generalized as an universal therapeutic principle and, more recently, as an educational maxim *par excellence*. But the problem was that the unconscious could not be denied or wished off. It returned in all kinds of devious ways. Jung attempted to make the unconscious of Freud a thing of personal beauty, but Rogers denied the demon entirely. There is a long history of such attempts at denial of the devil and they have all come to nought. While hysteria no longer abounds, the presence of schizophrenia in greater abundance than ever testifies to the presence and power of the unconscious primordial. No one cures schizophrenia—or much else psychopathological—without tackling the unconscious. And not to do so, is to deny the benefits of one's own creative resources, which are to be found in the unconscious.

The non-directive philosophy was always in a sense anti-intellectual while yet gathering to itself some of the greatest intellects of the time. Where Freud and Jung prized the value of a germinal idea, an image and a wish, and turned into scholars which would have done justice to a middle-ages monastic, non-directive therapy seemed to downgrade information and knowledge for feeling, and forced clients to feel rather than to think. This is of course overdoing it somewhat, but our critical point is sound. Psychoanalysis was always an intellectual as well as emotional task, and the aesthetics of the analytic situation was a kind of logical nicety which made peronality things fit for the patient. This was not just epiphenomenal but a central part of the cure for the experience of analysis was as important as its results. But therapeutic reorganization by brilliant people cannot simply rest with feeling and omit the cognitive/informational. In years of therapeutic practice, here are a few examples of decision-situations which our patients had to find solutions for:

54

1. A patient with a world-famous father discovered the idea of writing a personal book about him as a part of her therapy and which, to the book trade, was estimated to be worth about $500,000. Since her father was her therapeutic problem, the offer of a magnificent contract for such a book, when it came, put her into a deep therapeutic bind. . . .

2. A highly placed executive who had two surgical procedures on his spine—heavily freighted by psychosomatic aspects—was confronted by a third at a crucial point in therapy. He was told by his surgeon that if attempted, there was a 50% chance he might never walk again. . . .

3. A minister of a large church had had an unfortunate and momentary experience in which he had had undetected intercourse with a beautiful member of his parish in his church study. He was because of this full of guilt and considering leaving the church entirely after a lifetime of devotion. . . .

The relating of these therapeutic situations is not designed to imply that a directive therapist is needed to help the patient make the decision which, as it happens, is of unusual moment; it is simply to point up the fact that sometimes decisions which arise out of the therapeutic process are more than deciding which academic course to take or what subject to major in. They cannot be made simply on a will or clarification basis for the roots go very deep in the personality of the patient and if decided simplistically may change the entire life stream erroneously. We would not want to be personally responsible for such patients in which no recognition was given to buried masochistic, self-destructive and other aggrandizing unconscious needs.

Perhaps the greatest influence on the non-directive model was the failing medical model. Rogers, as a lay therapist, and similar to all therapists without M.D.s, was a little uncomfortable with the psychiatrists at the Rochester Clinic and early found unusual constraints anyway placed upon him by the medical model. Today radical psychiatry is saying much the same as what he fought for decades ago. What it amounts to is that the medical and growth models are not a unity and can never be one. Pathology has difficulty recognizing normality, lacks an ideal of the fully functioning person, and more or less contents itself with symptom or disease removal. In psychology, this has not turned out to be sufficient, nor is Everyman any longer satisfied merely to be free of dis-ease.

But in departing from the medical model it seems wise to amend it and not to destroy it. Ninety-nine percent of all people in the world are still healed under its auspices—even though they may chafe under it, they still want it. One can, for example, have no self-knowledge of undiagnosed tuberculosis or a brain tumor until a diagnosis is made. The will plays little part in it. No amount of non-direction can obviate or mitigate a brain tumor or whether or not one has schizophrenia, or the insult and directness of the information conveyed about it. Of course a non-directive approach can help the patient accept his condition and the possibility of a coming death. We suppose that a felt logical extension of the non-directive attitude might be toward death and dying, an area of great interest now by social scientists and therapists as well. This, as far as we know, has not yet been proposed.

It has always seemed to us that a logical outcome of the non-directive philosophy would be the evolvement and flowering of self-analytic techniques as envisaged early by Karen Horney. These would have been Western parallels to the self-growth arenas of Yoga, Taoism, Shinto and other great Eastern self-reflective movements. But self-analysis has been an essential failure in our world for reasons not yet clear. Perhaps it is that the yielding of a neurotic conflict involves the regressive need for a dyadic encounter with the Great Other so that both the aggression and love of crucial childhood experiences can be replayed. It is extremely difficult for the self to be both it-self and the Other at the same time. One cannot therefore self-analyze oneself in the same way in which the psychoanalyst does it. The resistances to the self it turns out are even greater than to the Great Other. Thus the trend of selfhelp through meditation, encounter groups, and the like leading to self-analysis has had a limited personal usefulness.

It was precisely because the Other in the dyadic relationship was feared that the non-directive placed so much stress upon the client for finding his own fate. Not only was this a distrust of authority, knowledge, symbol and myth, but a fearing of the soul of the Great Other. For a philosophy charged with attitudes of genuineness, empathy, and prizing others, the therapist became a suspicious object, until he could prove himself. But even beyond this, there was manifested in this approach an unwillingness to yield the self or ego to another for healing with the same faith one has in undressing when the physician asks you to. It seemed as though some God inside the patient would heal him, and the healer was merely a late comer to the scene. A genuine interpersonal healing does not have this phobic aspect and in longer-term treatment at any rate replicates the symbiotic trust of mother and child. The non-directivists could not offer that trust.

Perhaps more serious was the inadvertent happening that the non-directive philosophy set up *types* of therapists and placed valuations on them. In its earlier and formative phases directive therapists were felt to be if not misguided then evil men seeking their willful way. Students had a fear of becoming directive. But typologies, including those of Kretschmer, Spranger, Sheldon, Jung, and others have not in the history of scientific psychology led to a great deal.

All therapists we now know are both directive and nondirective. All therapists are client-centered or they would end up as bankers or in a similar vocation rather than as therapists. By life style, temperament, and design some therapists approach the core of the problem of their patients more swiftly and earnestly than do others. Some even shout, cajole, and command. But the point is this is done because either the problem or the patient requires it. No therapist worth his salt enjoys power for power's sake. No psychotherapy of schizophrenia, for example, can ever be attained without considerable direct intervention at certain moments of the treatment where life itself is at stake. There are certainly some patients who do better with a complete absence of therapeutic structure and direction, and others who insist on a maximum of it. The majority of younger patients for example refuse to free associate passively in the old way and want an actional/dialoging therapy. They resent passivity in the therapist and want motor behavior from him.

We must conclude that there are therefore no *types* of therapists, and no one type is privileged over another. There are instead only trained persons dedicated to helping patients in ways that come most easily to them and as the patient requires it. There is also no evidence that Ellis, Thorne, Rosen and similar others do not heal as rapidly and thoroughly as the non-directivists. Indeed, they claim just the opposite. The process of therapy is at any rate a matching of patient and healer and we do not yet understand how this works. And we only determine this matching empirically. Patients are not types either!

It is certainly clear that that therapy is best which intervenes the least and which maintains consciousness as the focus of its treatment. But no psychotherapist can deny the great power of the symbol, myth, and the primordial images of the unconscious which we put to healing use. Every well trained therapist will be both a non-directive and directive therapist on equally skillful levels, as his patient requires it.

CHAPTER VI

Adoration of the Patient and Its Disillusionment

ALL TEXTBOOKS ON PSYCHOTHERAPY assume that once the therapist learns to attain positive regard toward patients, he maintains it over a lifetime of practice. Of course, there are certain categories of patients which involve extreme difficulty in positive regard, for example, the chronic alcoholic, the character disordered, the drug addict; for many of us, positive therapeutic feelings for them are not there to begin with. But, by and large, such patients are not the stuff of everyday psychotherapy, and all but the minimally successful or specially motivated more or less bar them from the consulting room. The patients we are discussing here are the intelligent, subjectivistic verbalizers who symbolize and internalize their psychic pain and are mostly dependent on parent-surrogate models for amelioration. At any rate, the outcome of a formalized psychoanalytic/psychotherapeutic training, and the personal analysis which accompanies it, is a psychotherapist who can regard his patient comfortably and lovingly, and in such a milieu then apply the necessary corrective experiences which lead to the cure. Our long-time observations of the healers of schizophrenia: that is, psychotherapists of schizophrenia, reveal that, to the contrary of an almost universal belief, there may be a "burning out" or disillusioning process with therapeutic maturation and which seriously diminishes positive regard and may at times reduce it to zero.

Psychotherapists of schizophrenia are the most heuristic exemplars of disillusionment[1] possibly because of the dramatic and intense nature of their therapy. Treating schizophrenia is not so much an objective process, or even an artistic one, as an interpersonal involvement of great emotional moment. Objectivity or artistry can never provide the motor for the long years of intensive preoccupation required. These healers serve here as the raw data of a wider conception of the motivational curve of people who undertake to heal, and the application of healing energy to others. Healing schizophrenic patients represents many novel and unique facets of vocational choice which we want to briefly note in passing.

1. Schizophrenia is still considered a basically organic disease and thus refractory to the "talking cure."

2. It is impossible to have a classical tranference with a schizophrenic patient.

3. The patient can be dangerous and injure the therapist.

4. Schizophrenic communication consists of unsolved and unsolvable metaphors, symbols, and codes and reflect a brain or thinking disorder of considerable moment.

5. The patient's family will eventually undo the work of the therapist.

6. The treatment outcome, even if favorable, is never quite satisfactory, and seldom approaches a cure.

7. The patient makes demands on the therapist's time and person which are impossible to meet.

---

[1]Adoration and disillusionment are descriptive metaphors which while lacking in scientific precision gain in emotional impact in describing events in the transferential process which seem at times almost indescribable. As far as we know, they were first used in psychoanalysis by Searles.

8. The treatment method of choice is at any rate psychopharmacological or psychophysical, and functional analysis of conflict can only be secondary.

9. Administrators, and the hospital milieu, in general, disapprove of psychotherapy with schizophrenic patients because the upset which invariably occurs disturbs organizational procedures and personnel and thus defeats the hospitalized patient in the long run.

Despite these phobic therapeutic limitations in the psychotherapy of schizophrenia, there was a Harry Stack Sullivan and a Frieda Fromm-Reichmann, as a matter of record. Psychotherapy is done every day with schizophrenic patients, and psychiatric residents as well as highly experienced psychoanalysts tackle this form of illness. Some therapists are challenged to cure the incurable, "touch the untouchable;" but the vast majority of therapists flee from treating schizophrenia, giving as rationale, one of the above. Now it must be stated that anyone who devotes a lifetime to the specialty treatment of schizophrenias is open to the question of being a masochist or of having certain schizoid components himself! There are sufficient reports of the subjective treatment experience involved to reveal what a demanding, tortuous, frustrating, self-abnegating, and unprofitable activity this is.[2] The usual work-motives of power, pleasure, and monetary reward seem not to apply here, and the usual affluent-society goal of becoming Chairman of the Board can never occur here. What then induces a man to become a therapist of schizophrenia? The idea that the healer is a unique and dedicated person who gains his satisfactions by serving humanity is true, but it does not account for the fact that he serves in this particularly painful way. It seemed to us that such therapeutic work must perhaps be considered a "calling," similar to that which a priest receives "called" upon to serve God. Is it a kind of glory he seeks? Perhaps! But not of the

---

[2] See, for example, Will, O. A. Jr., "The Beginning of Psychotherapeutic Experience," in Burton, A. (ed.), *Modern Psychotherapeutic Practice.* Palo Alto: Science and Behavior Books, 1965.

kind priests or Congressional Medal of Honor winners receive.

It is our hypothesis that the compelling quality of being a therapist of schizophrenia is somehow rooted in the history of the therapist himself. By itself this is a trite statement, since all vocational choice has an element of personal history in it. However, we will try to show that the adoration (which is what it amounts to) of the schizophrenic patient has analogues in the adoration of one or another parent of the therapist, and the disillusionment and disinvolvement with the patient which invariably follows is comparable to the inevitable disillusionment with one's own parent in adolescence. The patient, so to speak, must represent certain aspects of the incomplete, unformed, inconsistent, poorly imprinted, or "bad" parent which were never worked through in the healer's psyche, and apparently not even in his own analysis. The schizophrenic condition itself represents an imperfect but *primary* form of existence, love, or agape which the healer himself needed but could not get, and which he now needs to complete his unfinished developmental work. Without it, there is always something lacking or questionable in his final individuation.

The natural history of a therapist of schizophrenia goes from healing the patient . . . to healing the family . . . to large scale research on schizophrenia . . . to the training or administration of other healers/hospitals . . . to "leaving the field" in one of five different capacities . . . we will argue that once the patient is healed[3] or, *per contra,* once he is demonstrated unhealable, the healer's own unconscious demons are quieted and his motivation toward healing schizophrenia declines. He feels tired, used-up, burnt-out—or verified, validated, liberated, etc.—and he goes on to other things and, for some, even suicide as a natural consequence.

Now, obviously, it would be crass to say that this is the entire healing story, or that it is the same with all therapists. We believe that much more is involved, for otherwise why

---

[3] The number of such patients which satisfies the need is as yet an unexplored variable. It has seemed to us to range from one case to more than a hundred.

wouldn't additional personal analytic work take care of it? The deep encounter with certain schizophrenic patients is of great and sublime magnitude and it is a position of personal privilege. It is as though the therapist were permitted to be present at the birth of creation and participate in it. It is personal feeling magnified to the 10th power, and it is the best proof that one is himself alive and loving. No experience such as this can merely serve as a therapeutic restitution or learning situation for it exists for itself, for its own ennoblement, and for its own growth-producing qualities.

To obtain the data which might substantiate or deny the above hypotheses, we sent a questionnaire containing the items below to 40 psychoanalysts or psychoanalytic psychotherapists who were known to us either through personal encounter and/or their writings. We do not know whether they are a representative sample of all therapists of schizophrenia, but the sample does contain a large number of the Sullivanian-trained group which specializes in the treatment of schizophrenia and is noted for it. Both medical and psychological (lay) practitioners are represented.[4] Twenty-seven of the 40 returned the questionnaire sent them, a significantly high number. In addition to this, we interviewed 10 Protestant ministers (in California) as a control group, to study the "call" they had experienced to enter the ministry and compare it with our therapists.

In this paper we do not attempt any statistical or mensurational approach to the data. The material is too personalistic for that. Any conclusion from this study must be considered merely heuristic. More elaborate designs will be required for a more objective follow-up.

The questionnaire was composed of the following items:

1. How did you happen to become a psychoanalyst/ psychotherapist rather than a surgeon, banker, publisher, corporate executive, etc.? Do you recall the essential conscious factors in your decision at the

---

4 Ph.D.'s in clinical psychology, plus personal analysis, plus at least 10 years' experience in healing neurotics and psychotics in institutional settings.

time? Retrospectively, what would you say were the unconscious dynamisms involved in such a choice?

2. What was the "pull" to work intensively with the most difficult disease of all—the schizophrenic illness of some duration? Are you aware of any less-than-conscious motivations which propelled you toward such challenge?

3. Have you found your dedication to psychotherapy (and particularly with the schizophrenic patient) to be cyclical, upwardly linear, in a uniformly diminishing curve, or a paroxysmally violent adoration and negation! Have you ever felt like giving up psychotherapy completely?

4. What peak or nadir experiences have you had in treating schizophrenic patients? (If you have already described this in some publication, please give the reference here as well.)

5. It has been said that to be successful with schizophrenic patients some degree of autism is necessary. Have you found that a deep communion with one's own unconscious, say, to the degree which Jung manifested it, is helpful?

6. We often talk of giving the patient love, and this seems crucial in the psychotherapy of schizophrenia. How would you describe the love you provide?

7. One hypothesis which has been proposed is that "omnipotence-based guilt" leads us to work with schizophrenic patients. This includes being overconscientious, sadistic, making the patient feel himself to be a burden, and in general placing him in a symbiotic situation in which our omnipotent and other needs are recognized. Can you comment upon this hypothesis insofar as your own experiences are concerned?

8. Analogies have been made in the literature between schizophrenia and death in the sense of calling schizophrenia a "walking death," etc. Has working with such patients challenged your feelings of Thanatos and Eros in any way? Do rebirth, resurrection, res-

cue, atonement and suffering fantasies play any part in your personality in this sense?

9. Do you at times feel the urgent need to resolve paradoxes, binds, and ambiguities?

10. The parameters of time/space are often said to be obtruded in encountering a challenging schizophrenic patient. Have you had such experiences?

11. What is the most acute experience of symbiosis which you have had? Has it been helpful?

12. The "human condition" is probably the best philosophical term which describes man's state of being-in-the-world. Do you feel inside or outside of that human condition?

13. It has been said that those who work with schizophrenics are more social scientists than biological ones. Do art, drama, and philosophy, etc., mitigate for you the possible aridity of the biological conception of the human being?

14. If you were selecting an ethical ideal for your escutcheon, would humanism rank high?

15. Please give seven adjectives which describe you (or use any other medium for giving a picture of yourself.)

From wider possibilities, this paper formally poses three essential questions:

1. Why do psychoanalysts/psychotherapists elect to become therapists of schizophrenia rather than bankers, publishers, senators, corporate executives, etc.?

2. How do therapists of schizophrenia perceive themselves as people and in relationship to their healing work?

3. Have they experienced an "adoration of the patient," and was there a subsequent disillusionment which followed?

Before systematically taking up these queries, we want to summarize some of the distinctive qualities of schizophrenia which are unmatched in the therapy of the neuroses, psychosomatic conditions, or other psychopathologies.

Primary Process: Nowhere does the primary process demonstrate itself as it does in schizophrenia. The Pandora's box which is the human unconscious suddenly disgorges so that delusion and hallucination, symbol and icon, take over the mental life. The psychic demons which most of us never have to confront directly are suddenly there to be coped with in schizophrenia. This is even painful to write about; but there is a movement in psychiatry which claims that the person more closely in touch with his primary process is mentally a healthier person. Jung spent most of his life attempting to receive and interpret messages from his unconscious,[5] and Laing[6] now holds seminars on the artificial psychotic experience as a contributor to personal growth. The rise of marijuana and LSD involve a similar need and, in fact, LSD was first believed to produce a temporary schizophrenia.

The primary process is thus an alchemical bridge to sensitivity and awareness and to more depthful interpersonal relationships. We have at times been astonished and even envied the schizophrenic for so glibly disclosing what we so carefully guarded over a lifetime. Schizophrenia thus mythologically offers up the riddle of existence which is so fundamentally contained in the unconscious.

Philosopher of Existence: We have in the past alluded to the schizophrenic as a poet. Artists, as we know, convey life messages from their unconscious to public awareness, and in this way assist in society's integration. We believe that the schizophrenic in some way fills a similar social role and which society requires. He is not just a sick person but a socially alienated and disenfranchised one as well. The schizophrenic and the hipster have much in common in that they are both

---

[5] Jung, C. G. *Memories, Dreams and Reflections.* New York: Random House, 1961.

[6] Esalen Foundation Program, Summer, 1968, Big Sur, California.

cultural dissidents, but each has his own unique phenomeno-logical defense for his faulted ego.[7]

When one does long-term psychotherapy with bright, frequently verbalizing schizophrenics, at the central core of their being are found the philosophical problems of existence which all men contend with. This is known as the human condition.

Every man tends to deny and evade critical existential issues by one and a thousand defenses, but the schizophrenic for some unknown reason cannot do so. He can only internalize, codify, dehumanize, and reflect them. He is a commentary on our times, a living example, as it were, of the penalties of civilized living. Underneath the autism, ambivalence, and perplexity is the real social question as to whether man can anymore love and be loved in return—whether or not he is to be devoured by his personal and social aggressions. The patient's perception of the nihilism and poverty of feeling extant today is acuter than ours and he acts upon it where we displace it. The metaphor of the schizophrenic, once it is decoded, poetically describes such human condition and the dilemma of man. It is as though to the madman has fallen the lot of pointing the way; it is from these patients that we learned about the facts of existentialism and not from Heidegger or Kierkegaard. The schizophrenic daily copes with bald ontic facts without dissimulation and out of this fashions his special kind of pathological freedom. Psychotherapy then becomes the demonstration that life with all of its binds and burdens is worth living.

The Cultural Rebel: Every cultured man is by definition hostile toward culture because he pays for acculturation with a part of his instinctual life. Culture binds man against his will to a set of moral principles which, while furthering the horde, is not always to his best interests.[8] Thus each man rebels against his cultural burden in one or another way. The schizophrenic is the rebel *par excellence* for he totally re-

---

[7] For the development of this argument, see Burton, A. et, al. *Schizophrenia as a Life Style.* op. cit.

[8] Rieff, P. *The Triumph of the Therapeutic.* New York: Harper & Row, 1966.

linquishes social responsibility and he, furthermore, has no apparent guilt about it.

If in some strange way everyone were magically to become schizophrenic, society would grind to a halt. The passivity experiences of Ghandi, Black sit-ins and other non-violent approaches to political life reveal that passivity constitutes a prime danger to society and greater than armed revolt. The schizophrenic is maximally passive and willing to die for his passivity. In this he is the greatest rebel of all and the most hostile of civilized men. It is not so much that the schizophrenic fears relatedness, but that he sees nothing worthwhile to relate to. Until he finds proper incentive he is content with the schizophrenic alter ego he constructs for himself. It is comparable to the heroin addict who has no social basis for resonance with the non-addicted middle-class acculturated psychotherapist and who cannot therefore make use of psychotherapy.

Secret of Thanatos: The great riddle of life is no longer birth but death. This is the supreme phobia of mankind. Certain forms of schizophrenia come close to "death in life" and because of this excite our interest. Most people secretly believe that it would be better to be dead than to be schizophrenic.

The psychotherapy of schizophrenia is a Lazarus-like affair in which the patient is resurrected. The microgenesis of those who have actually died and been resuscitated is not unlike the catatonic schizophrenic who once again accepts human existence and reports on it. Death is both a physical and psychic event, and the latter can precede the former as a separate event. Schizophrenia permits us to study death as a kind of laboratory event.

PART II

It can be expected that the usual lack of reliability in retrospective accounts of making an occupational choice will be improved by the fact that our sample of respondents all had personal analyses of one sort or another. This coupled with extraordinary verbal facility and a deep sense of looking inward should give greater credence to the motivational statements of our respondents. My queries troubled the respondents—as would be expected—and those who did respond did so with unusual vigor. Still, one's conceptions of one's motives must be taken with considerable salt, for we well know how the mind sees only what it needs to see. Be that as it may, the following represents the respondents' perceptions of why they became therapists of schizophrenia.

1. The conclusions of Henry[9] that members of the healing professions show distress in their early life is corroborated by our survey. The majority of therapists came from families in which a problem existed. Occasionally, this problem was a chronic physical disease which was disabling but which also had psychic overtones. Most often, however, it was a deep psychological involvement, with psychotic depression, schizophrenia, or even a serious character disorder. More than a rarity, relationships were in constant jeopardy and the majority of the family problems seem never to have been finally resolved. It is interesting that many of our therapists went out of their way to point out how emotionally helpful their spouses were to them, particularly in times of distress, and they considered their marital relationship as unusually blissful. This is curious because Henry again reports that for his therapists the healer's interpersonal closeness came largely from the office and not the home. This need to close marital ranks in our group may then be an overdetermined reaction to the ancient family disunity.

It seems plausible that just as one member of a family is unconsciously selected to be delinquent or schizophrenic, that is, the victim-martyr, another may be similarly picked to be the family healer. Tape recordings of the therapy of schizophrenic families bear this out. If, then, our therapist had imprinted in him the urgency to maintain family homeostasis, and he experienced difficulty in completing his assigned mission, he might well go to medical or graduate school to continue his efforts as a form of unconscious repetition com-

---

[9] Henry, W. E. "Some Observations on the Lives of Healers." *Human Development,* 1966, *9*, 47-56.

pulsion. Therapists of schizophrenia usually spend long, varied, and unpredictable hours with their patients, which of course cuts into time they can spend with their wives and families. The compelling needs of the patient often seem greater than the families', so that frequently a second or third, etc., marriage can be said to exist with the patient.

2. Identification with the maimed, the helpless, and the deprived is a well-known universal phenomenon. In athletic events, for example, the majority sentiment is always with the underdog. Our therapists have apparently been sensitized to the maimed and helpless for they identify more with them than does the layman. But this is not unusual for a service profession such as medicine, except that in this instance it is a true cathexis rather than a simple identification. Such cathexes assume an introjection of the helpless one, or rather a merging with him, so that the cure becomes as well a self-cure. There is a basic hidden rage in such professionals which drives the humanitarian effort. This is the rage of aloneness and the compensatory effort to dispel it. It easily becomes a life style, and if this happens the normal has little valence. This brings to mind the therapist who said that "he would rather treat than eat." Personal reward is to be found with the maimed and helpless for such a person.

3. One respondent said, "The hardest seems to me the most significant." Schizophrenia represents the frontiers of psychiatry—the single greatest problem still awaiting solution. Some of us are attracted by the impossible and still others cannot avoid it. The men who pioneered the West did not necessarily do so because of pecuniary need, but because their integration for a continuous challenge demanded it. Some personalities constantly require certainty; others regularly require uncertainty. Healing schizophrenia establishes one in his own eyes as having reached the pinnacle of therapeutic competency—of power and authority—of doing something which not even Freud and Jung could do. Having attained Parnassus, what later critique could possibly be taken seriously. And, indeed, one therapist of schizophrenia said that "it was the only way he could work without a supervisor on his back."

70

4. Jung's lifelong flirtation with his unconscious finds its counterpart in our therapists with the exception that it is someone else's unconscious they regularly delve into. In this sense, the therapist displaces his devilish forces to his patient and can in this way stop searching his own. The respondent who said that "Only in silence do we communicate," is interpreted to mean that two unconscious minds speak directly to each other, and silence is the royal road to liberation. The bizarre, the fanciful, the distorted, the fragmented, the displaced, had a fascination for our therapists. They felt a compelling need to track such states to their source. Malformation has its own reward. But what we think the therapist seeks in addition to his own demon is the fountainhead of creativity, the source of all inspiration and invention. The value of this to man would be even greater than finding Ponce de Leon's fountain of youth. One's creativity is also one's demon as most artists would testify. To be master of it is the greatest achievement of all and it gives what one healer described as a "clean feeling of honesty and meaningfulness . . . as opposed to a decided sense of cynicism I had been developing in the workaday world."

5. Our therapists generally denied that a symbiotic relationship existed with their patients at the same time they acknowledged abject dependency and helplessness on the patient's part toward them. They seemed fearful of admitting that they needed the patient in any way. One made it explicitly clear that the "love for his patient was not like the love he felt for his wife." Still, it is apparent that patient and therapist "feed off each other," and at momentary times cannot do without each other. If the "bad," double-binding or depriving maternal-model holds in the genesis of schizophrenia, then the corrective can only be a new remedial maternal source. This calls for some degree of temporary symbiosis, and the "mother" needs the child as much as the child needs the "mother." We have seen therapists who when administratively denied the opportunity of continuing the treatment of schizophrenic patients would quit their jobs. They would put the needs of the patient above that of the organizational order of the hospital. The need to be thera-

71

peutically intimate then takes this form of an extremely close relationship with the patient in which the needs of both participants are somehow served. Whether or not we label this symbiosis is not important.

6. There are people who flee from paradoxes, ambiguities, logical binds, myths, and symbols, and others who embrace them and seek them out. For one they represent an anxious time; for the other a challenge. In a certain sense, schizophrenia is the essence of the logical bind and symbolic ambiguity. Nothing really ever becomes clarified and nothing can be accepted at face value. Each percept or image invariably leads backward to an ambiguous or paradoxical situation which is seemingly without answer. The need to solve paradoxes and ambiguities of this kind is a metaneed of the therapist and schizophrenia becomes his laboratory. The need to reduce ambiguity is part of the source of creativity; the solving of the problem is the release of the self from tension and obsession it creates. And beyond this, insofar as culture itself involves absurdity and paradox, the therapist is provided with a mandate to reconcile social disparities. If he can solve the riddle of schizophrenia, he believes, then culture itself will yield to him.

The therapist of schizophrenia is a rare breed. He dares to tread where others fear to go, and the intensity of his devotion to the cause is unique. Does the interpretation of his motives to heal given above explain it? We would guess that there is one element lacking which needs now to be added. We were struck by the comment of one therapist that treating schizophrenia allows one to "track the symbol to its source." He adds, "It seems to me that the human being is just so much the product of symbolic events which characterize his life that it is all too easy for him to get caught up in a web of symbols." What we believe this therapist is saying is that *being* can be discovered through its symbols, and that it is necessary therefore to get to the root of symbolic being. Analysis is a process of successively reducing mental quanta to their lowest common denominator and applied to life it means discovering its sources. But on a psychic level we cannot seek explanations in terms of particles or enzymes

72

but rather in terms of the ontogenetic design of the individual. Assuming a basic drive toward existence, ontogenetic thrust, what form does it take in the individual life? This is more than a matter of style, for the style smacks of vogue and habit and insufficiently of the active choice of modes of being. Aloneness, a characteristic of our therapists, calls not only for distanciation, but for a bedrock intimacy which validates the values of aloneness. The normal fail to provide aloneness even if they would. In the schizophrenic one can witness the terrible joys and sorrows of existence and the devious road which aloneness takes. It is at best a pure observational and participational joy without the complexities of sexuality, housekeeping, child rearing, and marital games. Every therapist of schizophrenia has experienced this in the depths of treatment and it has ennobled him in regard to man and given him faith in him. To be present not at the birth of a life but at its creative design (and expression) is permitted to only the very few in society. The therapist is one of these and the fact that he becomes a therapist at all demonstrates his need to be present at such an event.

Therapists of schizophrenia have been variously described in the literature. Frieda Fromm-Reichmann thought that they were capable of giving the more than average love such patients required. We at one point called Marguerite Sechehaye and Gertrude Schwing, known for their treatment of schizophrenia, saint-like. In this study, we asked our therapists to describe themselves using seven adjectives. Here then are five responses gleaned from the total pool.

1. "Sympathetic, conscientious, sensitive, ambitious, energetic, tenacious, and grateful."

2. "Sincere, honest, brusque, libidinous, tough, erotic, and tender."

3. "An extroverted introvert, thoughtful, homeloving, curious, critical, perfectionistic, and tolerant."

4. "Aggressive, ambitious, impatient with personal limitations, vacillating in mood when reacting to the

73

latter, generally content, zest for life, periodically self-critical."

5. "Friendly, reserved, optimistic, hardworking, tolerant, 'giving,' mildly nihilistic, and self-indulgent."

Henry again quotes "research and popular lore" as descriptive of the healer personality as having "intense and commonly vicariously-met needs for personal contact, to be late and often turbulent sexual maturers, more hysteric than normal, to have strong but conflictive ties with their families," in other words, some manifestations of neurotic personality. While our therapists frequently admit to neurotic tendencies, they do not actually see themselves this way. If anything, they are sustained and unvarying in their basic tenacity, in their direct experience of life, and in a certain stable sensitivity to existence. They are islands unto themselves, reserved, but internally pioneering. Essentially they are symbolists rather than activists, and images and feelings are the stuff of their lives. They are capable of tolerance and tenderness and are, above all, sincere and sober about life. Depression and the periodic flight of creativity is the problem they most frequently recognize in themselves.

A special item must now be mentioned. The greatest defeat some of our therapists have experienced, as they report it, is the suicide of a patient they have worked with for years. And, as well, the persistent refusal of a long-term schizophrenic patient to grow with treatment. Such poignant feelings about treatment in this area can only come to people for whom life has a special meaning. To call it humanitarian would be limiting the question. It is rather that a person's life is considered a treasure—*the treasure*—and the purpose is to live it fully. Any fixation, inhibition, repression, delusion, etc. defeats this ontic purpose and must be changed. The death of a patient by suicide who is coming to such fruition is felt by the therapist as the Sophoclean tragedy of psychotherapy.

It is indicative that most of the therapists in our study were no longer actively treating schizophrenics at the time of completing the questionnaire, but were doing research on schizophrenia, chairing Departments of Psychiatry in various university medical schools, heading sanatoria, training others in methodology, or treating non-schizophrenic patients. A vast majority admitted to having had feelings of giving up therapy, leaving psychiatry or psychology, and moving on to calmer waters. Their devotion to therapy, they agree, is cyclical and, with very rare exceptions, as they age they tend to see fewer and fewer schizophrenic patients. They have become disillusioned! Below are three insightful responses to this area of experience.

1. "Definitely cyclical." (Dedication to healing schizophrenics.) "Now, I do psychotherapy for my personal satisfaction since I can gain more status and rewards from writing and research. I also think I can have more impact and do more good on a broader scale by writing and research. For me, psychotherapy has become somewhat of a selfish pursuit mainly justifiable for my own enjoyment. Especially is this true of schizophrenics since objectively they rarely achieve great things in life. I could personally justify my time better seeing creative productive people who do influence in some way the world about us. I no longer work with socially inadequate regressed schizophrenics because for me it just isn't worth it; after a great personal investment and time commitment to see a patient markedly improve and then because of age and lack of education be only a dishwasher and live at essentially a poverty level is deeply upsetting—for myself life would be so unfulfilling that I might rationally choose suicide to such an existence."

2. "I have never been close to giving up psychotherapy all together, but have often entertained the idea. My work with schizophrenic patients was most enthusiastic in my early years, during my residence training and for about 10 years thereafter. The tremendous discouragement of slow movement in schizophrenics, and often no evidence of movement, gradually pushed me in the direction of working with families instead of with individual schizophrenic persons. In the family interaction, especially between husband and wife, I experience some

of the same high voltage and profound stirring that I formerly sought in the work with schizophrenics."

3. "My dedication to psychotherapy has been cyclical but I do not think I could describe it as paroxysmally violent in adoration aspects. I have, at times, become restless about the tremendous amount of commitment that must be made in order to work successfully with schizophrenics. I tend to have a somewhat depressive-hypomanic nuclear problem in my own personality and I think at times when I was somewhat hypomanic, I found it very difficult to work with schizophrenics and was much more interested in those periods in doing administrative and organizational psychiatry. In these instances I programmed the work of others, rather than working with patients intensively myself. I would say somehow that I would tend to work in a clinical way psychotherapeutically with schizophrenics perhaps when I had either a relatively good baseline or perhaps was slightly depressed. I have on rare occasions felt like giving up psychotherapy completely. During such periods I have seriously questioned whether psychotherapy can be of value to anyone, but these periods have been brief. For the most part I believe that psychotherapy has promise, including psychotherapy with schizophrenia."

Disillusionment is inherent in all maturational processes in which growth is the requirement. One becomes disillusioned with parents, marriage, children, friends, society, etc. Illusions about the interpersonal consist of expectation of maximal love and succorance and when these become sated or are less than ideal the illusions become disabused; i.e., they are dis-illusioned. The therapist expects growth and humanity from his patient, in a manner similar to the description above. If he never finds it, he becomes disillusioned. But indeed this happens more often when he does find it. As therapist and patient grow and become more identical they need each other less and less, and they come to see each other differently. A frequent outcome of such growth is the attempt on the part of the patient to change the relationship to a sexual or marital one. By then, therapeutic disenchant-

76

ment has totally set in. Thus a therapist preconsciously hates to see the schizophrenic patient grow up in the way one regrets a child growing up and leaving home. But one would not want to forego the adoration experience because of the certainty that it will end some day—disillusioned.

The therapist needs to adore someone in a way he doesn't find—and cannot find—at home actually or historically. He needs to participate in the miracle and mystique of existence in the primal way offered only by the psychotic patient. In this he not only integrates himself and finds his joy, but satisfies the therapist role with which he was imprinted by his early family experience. We found it somewhat different with the ministers who looked to their godhead for salvation rather than to their flock.

Since love seems to be the currency of the healing of schizophrenia, we asked our healers what it was. This is how they replied.

1. "Love is consistency, full attention, remembering and repeating statements made by the patient."

2. "A schizophrenic man asked me, 'Do you love me?' After squirming verbally and non-verbally for 10 minutes, I told him what I felt for him was not the same feeling I had for my wife or my children but I did not hesitate to call it love. This resolved an impasse in therapy."

3. "I would rather disagree with the idea of giving the patient love as essential to the treatment of schizophrenia . . . One must not need the patient; and I think giving love must be related to some need for the patient. Respect, concern, continuing interest are important—and perhaps even affection."

In this chapter we have tried to show, using the schizophrenic patient, that all psychotherapy is a process of analogical adoration and disillusionment mirroring the growth process in life itself. It could be no other way.

77

CHAPTER VII

The Therapist as Patient

SINCE PSYCHOTHERAPISTS ARE THEMSELVES HUMAN, and thereby subject to the same psychic disturbances as their patients, it happens more than infrequently that they have to apply for psychotherapy in the same way as do their patients. At the same time they are receiving psychotherapy they of course continue to offer it to others. Perhaps it is because we are senior members of the psychotherapeutic profession and have written a number of books on the topic that we have apparently attracted more than our share of such therapist-patients.[1] It is because over the years we have been more or less dissatisfied with the outcomes of such treatment work that we felt impelled to write this chapter as a way of coming to terms with our dissatisfaction. Possibly our work with therapist-patients has not really been so bad, for we have a tendency to expect perfection in therapists, but at any rate our experiences with these very special patients may be helpful to others who treat therapists.

We want to make clear before going on that the therapist-patient discussed in this chapter does not come for training purposes or for certification, although this may be a peri-

---

[1] To avoid an inherent terminological confusion, we will henceforth call the psychotherapist who comes for treatment the *therapist-patient* and the one who provides it the *therapist*.

pheral value to the experience. They were all hurting badly and needed help to continue to function in their customary way. Most had already had psychoanalysis or personal therapy as a part of their earlier training, but for others this was the first experience as a patient. It seemed to make little difference to their current patient status, insofar as we could tell, whether they had had or had not had such preparatory analytic work.

There are major resistances to a therapist seeking help from a colleague and he may drag on for years before implementing the decision to actualize such help. There are also different resistances which become apparent after the therapist-patient has called the healer and had an interview with him. The most vital of these prologomenon resistances is that the therapist-patient sees his image as a therapist internally damaged by needing to apply for such help. Most of us—perhaps because we are in continuous demand as therapists—have the smug inner feeling that we can never really become psychotic, or even severely neurotic, because our patients need us and because we do help them. We believe it is important to have such a feeling of immune confidence to be an effective therapist for whatever the literature, for example, says about the "cured schizophrenic" making the best therapist of schizophrenia, there is always the preconscious uneasiness in the therapeutic supervisor that the "cured one" may regress to the primordial under unknown and special stress. The best professionals have a kind of confidence and arrogance not warranted by reality, and a part of such confidence is that they do not fall heir to the diseases they treat. Should this perchance happen, they can become sad psychological cases indeed.

There are also varying amounts of shame and guilt in becoming a patient, residuals of certain 19th century stigmata, but still very much in covert evidence.[2] Such therapist-pa-

---

[2] Once a therapist has gone to a colleague for something as elemental as a marital problem, we have noted that the public relationship between the two is somehow altered despite the strongest intentions for it not to change on the part of both. The most startling indicator is that the regular patient referral relationship changes between the two.

tients have as well a mortal fear of meeting other and regular patients in the waiting room and demand more than their share of covertness in treatment. Practically, the need to protect one's reputation for business purposes cannot be denied. Carl Rogers is both unique and courageous when he describes going to one of his own students for therapeutic help at a time of crisis in his life. While we extoll the openness of getting help, few of us are as yet able to dispell the residual barriers which exist in making therapy a virtue.

A second barrier, discussed in somewhat greater detail below, is what we call the "disturbance of faith dynamics." Physicians, for example, are notorious for not following their own prescription when they personally become ill. What is indicated for their patients is not necessarily indicated for them, as they interpret it. Knowing the inside and convolutions of medicine, including the deficiencies of its personnel, they cannot but maintain a certain skepticism about medicine, which only a total faith abridges, and which they demand from their patients. The therapist-patient knows that a respectable number of scientists, and those in good faith, believe that psychotherapy is no more effective than chance or self-reparation, or that it may even do harm, and that its practitioners, as a group, furthermore fall a little short of the Aesculapian ideal. Such questions, formerly safely "tucked away," now become obsessive and deter him from becoming a patient.

Thus it is that the therapist-patient comes to treatment only when his total personality structure is seriously threatened in some way. Such threatening situations incarnate themselves into the following behavioral manifestations as exemplars.

1. The therapist-patient is threatened with the loss of his wife. We have pointed out elsewhere that the wives of therapists serve very special functions in the lives of their husbands and therapists can hardly do without them. When the marriage works, the wife almost becomes the therapist's Other: his source of id satisfaction, his friend, his lover, his colleague, and, the wives believe, his "own therapist without portfolio."

The relationship is almost embarrassingly close and dependent. This is to be distinguished from the "office marriage," which differs by being idealized in place of sexualized, fantasied instead of realized, transferred rather than lived. So the imminent loss of a loved and useful wife, for any reason, is of the greatest moment to the therapist-patient and will often force him to seek therapy.

2. The therapist-patient is threatened with the loss of self. Most therapists live more closely to the unconscious or perhaps even to psychosis than do other people. They court this kind of special state by being vocationally involved with it every single day, and both Freud and Jung and similar others had their specific episodes of psychotic-like strangeness. But therapists are extremely fearful of becoming psychotic partly, we suppose, because they know first hand of its grimness, boredom, and social impossibility.

When anxiety approaches panic, when mood becomes melancholy, when aggression becomes (imaginal) murder, when love becomes incestuous, when heterosexual becomes homosexual, etc., then the therapist-patient begins to fear psychosis and is impelled to do something about it. It may be that a drug experience or an encounter group intimacy or a love affair shakes his self-foundations, but whatever the stimulus he becomes basically afraid of losing the parameters of self.

3. When a loss of ontic thrust and therapeutic conviction arise in the therapist-patient's own treatment work, he becomes frightened and saddened at his inability to maintain his work-motivation edge. This can often be described as a form of depression, but it actually goes beyond depression. Where formerly each day was met with a special zest—looking forward to the challenge of the quotidian patients—now the day is grey and a herculean effort is required to mobilize oneself. Where each day is itself the personal affirmation of a set of values, and a specific life-style, now they suddenly are found strangely wanting. Depression is mostly a matter of history, but this kind of impasse is more a loss of intercurrent thrust and the denudation of the life-tokens which let us get through each and every day. The basic postulates of life, the philosophy of existence, for some strange reason re-pre-

81

sent themselves for additional reflection and evaluation when they have already been incorporated into the corpus of the personality and successfully motor it. All of this brings a special quality of helplessness, terror, and anger to the therapist-patient of which the extremest adjustments are images of suicide or homicide.

4. Most distress to the therapist-patient occurs when his parapraxes (slips) start showing to his own patients. We have done this ourselves and know the amazement, chagrin, and discomfiture it provides particularly when sensitive patients start interpreting them. Therapists rarely make parapraxes when giving interpretations. Should they occur it reveals the growing conflict in the therapist-patient, but more than this, that his unconscious is "slipping" out of his grasp. Fall from grace on the part of their therapist-model is both frightening to patients but very much desired by them. They can then get an unexpected quantum of guilt-reward. If the patient also gets the idea that his therapist needs personal help, he will step into the breach and try to heal him. This more than all else destroys the therapeutic relationship for the healing and to-be-healed roles then become inextricably confused. Therapists furthermore have considerable investment in not becoming patients in their treatment work, defending vigorously against it, so that under such circumstances the entire faith and trust situation of psychotherapy becomes altered.

The above are only a few of the possibilities which bring the healer to patient status. How then does he go about finding his therapist? What guides him in the search for the person who can help him under the conditions of fear and resistance? The whole question of how one selects a helper is so tenuous and so evanescent that little objective can really be said about it. One would expect that being a therapist some fundamental insight into the personality of therapists, or at least into the process itself, would aid in making such choice. This hardly seems the case. The selection of a therapist by other therapists is made on a dynamically preconscious or unconscious basis and then rationalized in terms of a few qualities. Of course, knowledge and technical proficiency are cited with great frequency. A great number of our therapist-patients have come citing something we said in an article or book to which they responded on a depthful and personally meaningful level. Sometimes this was an innovative thing, and for others some peculiarity or strength in our personality they had seen or heard about. Charisma still counts for much everywhere. Even sophisticated therapists are attracted to, even admire, the social presentation of self which is the grand flourish, the imprimatur of worldliness and know-how. Freud, Jung, and Charcot were in great demand for this reason and there is no evidence that they were technically great healers on a day to day basis.

And the choice of therapist must involve a man who is above the din of psychiatric battle. By this we mean that the politics of psychotherapy are for our therapist-patients best left by the wayside for he does not want his therapeutic work to encroach on academia, publications, growth centers, and his operative arena. The therapist who has "made it," who is no longer seeking power or affluence, who can take the time to reflect on the human condition, who has resolved the major dilemmas of his own life, etc., is the one sought out. Of course, this is the father archetype, *par excellence,* or rather the Wise Old Man, in Jung's sense.

But above all, the therapist chosen must be in the therapist-patient's own image, or must at least be capable of being idealized as such. Our psychological ontogeny is that one must recapitulate the phylogeny of Sigmund Freud, or in his absence a reasonable apostle. Coming to psychotherapy is coming to the historical Freud, and the resolution of conflict must be consanguinous with the image of mastery. All such patients are existentially concerned with squeezing the last drop of joy out of life, and with converting work into pleasure. And, was this not Freud's final message?

Once in therapy the therapist-patient has an alert watchfulness which seems to go beyond that of other patients. We often feel that we are on probation. They are not so ready or willing to enter a deep transference, and they often rubber-stamp the word "reservation" on any interpretation offered them. Of course, this is not the case in every instance, and a great deal depends on the specific therapeutic dyad. A dilemma which arises early is whether one should treat the therapist-patient as a colleague or as just another patient? If one does the former, one acknowledges a special parenthood status, a sharing of technical niceties, and agrees that this is a temporary and extraordinary event. In the second instance a more indifferent objectivity governs. We have done it both ways and have reluctantly concluded that it benefits no one to exempt the therapist-patient from full patient status. He can be given no exemption from a process which permits none.

Before we go into methodological matters by which such treatment work may be furthered we want to summarize the major resistances with which therapists will have to cope in such specialized patients.

1. It is a paradox that those therapists who are most firmly convinced of the efficacy of psychotherapy and, indeed, spend their entire professional lives immersed in it, are also precisely those who have the most fundamental and deeply-rooted doubts about it. The professional therapist is also a realist about psychotherapy and is familiar with the oft-quoted statistic of "one cured, one helped a little, and one helped not at all or made worse." But, beyond this less than perfect outcome, he even (periodically) has doubts whether therapy works at all, whether it isn't perhaps a pure construct fantasy, or whether it isn't the purchase of friendship at best. The mass media, his nonclinical friends, and even most of his non-psychiatric scientific colleagues accept his work with a certain cynicism or amusement.

All such doubts are successfully kept at bay until the therapist himself falls prey to severe anxiety, guilt, and conflict, and then his doubts come back in force to hound him. Many leave the field at this point. There is an ego difference in subjecting others to a life/death therapeutic struggle and being the object of that struggle oneself. This reminds us of the physician we once had in therapy who mentioned that he took antibiotics intensively at the first sign of a cold. When we suggested that this went counter to the usual medical prescription for antibiotics, he agreed, but said that in this instance his *own* life was involved. And, we have said, the greater the original conviction of efficacy and resolution, the greater the doubt. Charisma, assuredness, and conviction, when precipitously emptied of content, fall into a nothingness. The faith dynamics which underlie every single cure of record become penetrated or shattered by inside process information, and faith irrevocably works to gloss over the weaknesses, deficiencies, and inadequacies of the healing process. The internecine warfare between psychoanalysis, client-centered psychotherapy, behavioral modification, rational-emotive therapy, encounter group approaches, and similar others is precisely the need to keep the important inside questions circumscribed. It seems that doctrinaire heretics are burned at a whiter heat than the garden variety of apostate.

It is fruitless to try to reconfirm the basics and elementals with the therapist-patient who is now attacked by such doubts. The fact that he is there at all means that the positive outweighs the negative and that his faith in himself can be expected to be reinstated sooner or later. If his psychotherapy life-style is seriously in question then one may have suicidal material to contend with and it may be a problem of a different order. We content ourselves in the first instance with being an exemplary model of the helpfulness of therapy, philosophize at times about its place in the human condition and in human growth, and stand firm in what we know it can do and what we have done with it. We refuse to be taken over by the doubts, acknowledging in this way the limits of our therapeutic knowledge, but referring the doubts more directly to the personal process and to the intercurrent situation. We ask for and usually receive the temporary suspension of rational criticism which all people who become patients must offer in some degree or other. But, it must be admitted, being a professional makes it more difficult to again become a tyro.

2. Few of the original Vienna psychoanalytic circle had psychoanalyses, and the master of course analyzed himself. Therapist-patients believe that what was good enough for

Freud is good enough for them. The therapist-patient carries on a self-analysis at the same time he is having an other-analysis. That is, his "third ear" which is always busy analyzing, gestalting, and shoring up is treating his ego, and the help of the Other is demanded only when it fails him. When it again becomes capable, the Other is relinquished.

Whether we like to think of it this way or not, our usual patients are not only healed by us but heal us in turn. By this we mean that the daily contact with them is reinforcing of values, styles, awareness, and mental content. Without them, we might at times be in existential difficulties. More than we are aware their treatment provides support, insight, and growth for the therapist, which is perhaps why all patients at some stage in the process want to become healers too. The ultimate relationship between patient and therapist is closer than between therapist and non-patient. The symbols and archetypes of the unconscious, closer to the surface in the identified patient, are universally healing, and their formulation and expression in therapy heals all participants. When the therapist-patient feels that his therapy is far enough along to be returned to his own self-analysis status, and to the help of his own patients, he stops treatment.

3. The therapist-patient wants basically to treat himself, not necessarily as self-analysis, but in momentous dyadic dialogue. His self-image and narcissism are such that he is for himself the primal therapist, and he feels his self-knowledge and humanity are just a shade above that of other therapists. The fact that being his own therapist has failed him is wished off on one ground or other. For this reason the transference is always difficult, if not seriously incomplete, with therapist-patients. The ability to transfer is the ability to go back in time, to surrender family power, and to be willing to nurse again at the breast. Therapist-patients are ever fearful of personal regression, and they also want to leave their still unresolved family romance strictly alone, clothing it in a romantic aura. Some even have the illusion that it is all safely behind them.

This wanting to be one's own therapist interferes with the dynamics of *interpretation* which Freud found so useful. An interpretation is not merely a cognitive operation but a gestalt set in an emotive framework. People interpret all the time; but what carries a growth factor with it is that the wish, symbol, or image interpreted rearranges the past and future interpersonal structure into a new moment of greater hope. The interpretive bill of lading must be existentially useful for otherwise the interpretation has no *force majeure* behind it. The emotion of oneness rarely has the same impact as the emotion of "twoness," the psychic joining of what was once a biological or cosmic unity, and so becoming one's own therapist rather than a willing patient evacuates the affect of interpretation and reduces its quality—sometimes to nothing.

4. We have hypothesized earlier that the therapist's father rather than his mother was critical in his becoming a therapist. The father was actually idealized, invariably successful, given to long absences from the home, indifferently related to his spouse, and was part of a problem home from which he distanced himself. The mother tended to be drab, non-creative, self-indulgent, indifferently loving, and interfering in the relationship between father and son. Becoming a therapist for such a boy then became an unconscious process of replaying the family romance which was never completely tackled in the training or personal analysis or later along the line. It was a search for the introjected but absent father.

In psychotherapy, the therapist becomes not a mother but a father, which would help explain the puzzling social fact that most patients in psychotherapy are women and most therapists men. It also clarifies to some extent the heavily weighted love and sex content of the therapeutic process.

Be that as it may, when a therapist-patient comes into treatment he is seeking a transferential mother and not a father. In his own work he is the powerful father, identifying totally with his own father whom he never quite got enough of, and offering this model to his own patients. But when he is in personal trouble, the castrating competition with a male father-healer in treatment is so arousing and so conflicting with the role he has introjected for himself that resistance inherently comes to the treatment and, in fact, the more powerful the therapist the greater the resistance. The question then arises why the therapist-patient doesn't apply to a woman healer for help? The answer seems to be that they are at any rate not in great abundance, and they furthermore lack a certain needed charisma and power in a field given over almost entirely to men. In our work with such therapist-patients we have found that "coming on strong," even when such strength represents a brilliant *tour de force* of treatment, is violently resisted by the therapist-patient and precisely when he is aware of the appositeness of the procedure or interpretation. He then more than ever puts his knowledge in the service of resistance.

Not much good is done by trying to become mother instead of father in such situations because the role-playing is partly fraudulent in terms of the therapist's unconscious. Of course, the treatment can be kept supportive and ego, so that these factors do not arise with such great force. One can avoid the intense transference entirely. But this often defeats precisely what is needed by the therapist-patient; that is, the harmonizing of the male and female principles, the father and the mother, the Yin and the Yang. What we have done in situations like this, as we explain in greater detail below, is to assume a gestalt treatment approach. That is, we become more like Fritz Perls than ourselves. Since we have had a great deal of encounter group experience, even collected a book on the topic, this is not so difficult as it might be for others. What it amounts to is that for the purpose of treating the therapist-patient we put psychoanalytic pyschotherapeutic concepts (and techniques) temporarily in limbo and approach the treatment as an *in vivo* thing between two knowledgeable and psychologically sophisticated people. We become a sort of "wild therapist" for the purpose of his growth. And it works. The younger therapist-patients particularly like this, are more familiar with encounter principles, less afraid of it, and they then can put their knowledge in the service of healing rather than resistance. But in doing this we haven't for one moment surrendered Sigmund Freud.

5. The final inhibitor to therapy of this kind is shame. There is a kind of damage that is done to a therapist-patient

when he is forced to become a fellow sufferer of those he regularly treats that is so subtle and intangible as to defy description. Many of us feel shame—even anger—for those of our patients who offer consistent long-term helplessness and dependency. Sometimes the idea of cowardice-as-neurosis even enters the mind. And we must not forget that the history of the treatment of the neuroses is one of some aggression and violence. The difference between a patient and a therapist is much greater than the fact that one lies on the couch and the other sits behind it. There is an invisible line, perhaps best exemplified by the act of being admitted to the state mental hospital, which once crossed changes something basic in the social arrangement of things, in the person, and in his milieu. Having observed patients enter and leave such hospitals for about two decades convinces us that not social stigmata are involved but rather the most complex inhibitors of self-facilitation. Successful ego-functioning is always a balance of talent and the uncertain image of that talent but which at any rate leads one to take outstanding chances against social odds. The social climate is such that it perpetually inhibits new creative forms and gestalts, and the self has to counter this cultural force.

One such ego-starter, as we call them, is the self-image of intactness, of vitality, of self-reparation. Tomorrow will always be a new start, a better day, a new opportunity for those chances missed today. The entire biological function, its moods and tides, is based upon this inherent and unified continuity of strength, which if broken, the organism often goes into a quick decline, and sometimes to death. A therapist becoming a patient of yet another therapist, the theory of its aesthetics aside, is apparently one of those subtle damages which inhibits the ego, breaks the biological continuity, and reduces the ego's "starting" power. Why this should be so psychologically, for it does not univocally follow from physical medicine, is not exactly clear. But it would seem generically that some helping situations are also damaging ones; or put another way, all help brings with it a quantum of entropy. The ego of the therapist is so carefully balanced in reality and vital mythology that any improvident redefini-

89

tion-attempt sets it teetering. If my ego is a helping ego, and if I see people all around me who need my help, and who spontaneously come to me for it, then I cannot all of a sudden see my ego as a needing-to-be-helped ego. Should· this suddenly be forced upon me by specific and incontrovertible life circumstances, then the revaluation of self which occurs will have to include as extreme possibilities psychosis, suicide, or simply wasting away into some form of existential limbo or other.

If we have been successful in clarifying what the situation of therapist turned patient means dynamically, then we can more easily move on to how therapy may best proceed with this kind of patient. The situation is not as grim as the various resistances we have described would seem to make it. If Ellis[3] is correct on the values of rationality, then therapist-patients ought to proceed faster in treatment. Similarly, while the transference aspects rarely seem as intense with these patients as with others, on symbolic and archetypal levels the potency of the therapeutic encounter outranks the generic patient. Also, we believe much more healing goes on *between the hours* with therapist-patients than it does with other patients. More healing also takes place symbolically after the treatment has stopped as well. Depression gives way to life, and integration occurs more quickly than with others. An aggrieved wife who wants to leave may then be more easily replaced by another woman by the therapist-patient, or a transferential relationship with a female patient may temporarily become a stopgap as a part of one's regular function. The pull of Thanatos is shelved because a vital work remains to be done and the biological/life unity, the wholeness of existence, is more quickly reinstated.

PART II

There is perhaps no one best way to treat a therapist-patient. The following observations have evolved over years of such work, but we can't say that they are the last words.

---

[3] Ellis, A. *Growth Through Reason.* Palo Alto: Science and Behavior Books, 1971.

1. Regardless of the symptom picture offered, the therapist should count on a short-term period of treatment. This is true even if the question of a marginal or borderline psychosis is involved. Some of the reasons for this have already been stated. It remains simply to say that the vast majority of therapist-patients want only a quick rescue service, an opportunity to quickly reintegrate, a support for faltering philosophical or existential perspectives, and an opportunity to return to their healer life style. They are at any rate impatient with the lengthiness of psychoanalysis or psychoanalytic psychotherapy and the impatient impression they give is that they would rather "go down the drain" than submit to a two or three year term of analytic treatment. They know that their own healing mechanisms and resources have temporarily failed them, and they want only the opportunity to re-start them no matter how grossly. There are exceptions, of course, but the uniformity of this finding in our patients has been astonishing.

The tension between the therapist-patient's need for short-term treatment and the therapist's frequent perception of the need for a longer-term relationship sets up a conflict, and which in fact motivated the writing of this article. But we have since concluded that the therapist-patient was correct. While the elegance—and outcome—of a longer-term therapy are perhaps greater, the patient does indeed choose what he wants to do with his life even though *we think he should know better*. There is a certain governing economy about biological/social life which sets its own existential level, even though it appears at times to be at an excessive cost, and this principle of life is tampered with at the therapist's and patient's peril. We now do treatment with therapist-patients from moment to moment, from hour to hour, from day to day, secure in the feeling that of all our patients the therapist-patient is the best qualified to work out his own fate, and that we are only there to help him do it—not do it for him.

2. A gestalt rather than analytic type of therapy is indicated with most of these patients. By this we mean that the therapy offered healers must be more synthesizing than an-

91

alyzing, more therapeutically active than passive, more momentary than historical, more phenomenologically emotional than studied, more expressive than rational, more confronting than sustaining, more impulsive than regulative, etc. This is anyway what the younger counselors and therapists mostly believe in. Such novel approaches do better on the short term, and at any rate have their own mostly adequate healing rationale.[4] They are peculiarly apposite here in that they more quickly aid restitution, provide conflict-relief, and ego and intellectual modes of adjustment. "Doing something" rather than doing it in fantasy or symbolically, or spending major energy in the intricate analysis of motivational meaning, seems more indicated here than with other patients. This is, of course, not to say that we throw our entire treatment bag out the window for much of it is still strictly conventional.

3. Paradoxically, more listening is indicated with therapist-patients than with other patients. Therapists have to listen so much that they wait patiently to someday "tell their story." Letting them do so is probably the single most curative thing of all. We thus have the interesting treatment situation in which the therapist is both more active but says less. Listening is a kind of activity which, under gestalt therapy principles, becomes a dynamic vehicle for change. And, in fact, therapist-patients, in their immediate desperate need, interrupt the therapist more than other patients, and seem not to allow as much exposition on his part. They seem to be saying, "Just listen to me and I'll be all right . . . there is nobody I can tell it all to but you."

4. We exaggerate the modeling properties of the therapeutic process with therapist-patients. By this we mean that we use ourselves more as therapy than we do our words, symbols, or processes. By our presence, we reaffirm the values of existence, the life-style of the therapist, and the prospects of a highly positive outcome of our work together. We show the therapist-patient by modeling that life is worth living,

---

[4] Burton, A. (ed.). *Encounter. The Theory and Practice of Encounter Groups.* San Francisco: Jossey-Bass Publishing Co., 1967.

that it has at least one peak experience every day, and that we try to live it fully and in no other way. We also tell him of the time we too had to become a therapist-patient.

While therapist-patients can in their special state ignore, delimit, or extinguish an analytic interpretation, they cannot so easily dismiss the evidence of the viable therapist. It is not so much what the therapist says as what he is that has effects on such patients. Therapists are very sensitive to the inner life of others, and so they are similarly to that life in their therapist. Should they ever find it faulty, deficient, or dishonest, they would not return to treatment. But, contra, its observed vitality and existential pleasure are curative.

5. It would be expected that since the therapist-patient is treating cases while he is being treated he would be interested in ego-analogues which are in a sense case examples. Alcoholics Anonymous, Synanon, Daytop, and similar group organizations succeed primarily because the "cured" example is never very far out of sight. We have to some extent used this technique in general psychotherapy,[5] but here it finds a more proper place. Without giving names, we offer brief sketches of problem situations and how they have responded to our therapeutic auspices. Many times we use facets out of our own life. Usually, this approach is a rare procedure, and only where a major resistance is involved. But the therapist-patient cannot ignore this for by virtue of his life-style he is also on the prowl for case examples. He cannot, therefore, refuse to apply such examples to his own life.

6. Psychotherapy is not by any means limited to the therapeutic hour. To account for the interval effects in treatment in variegated clients, we previously offered the concept of interval therapy.[6] Our experience has been that therapist-patients accomplish a lot more in between hours than do others. To encourage this we ask the patient if he will assume certain activities away from the hour. This may involve painting, sculpting, keeping a journal, a diary, or similar self-crea-

---

[5] Burton, A. *Interpersonal Psychotherapy. Op. Cit.*
[6] Burton, A. *Modern Humanistic Psychotherapy. Op. Cit.*

tive work. He brings it to the session in the way we have described in an earlier book.[7]

Most therapist-patients have not had experience with this modified Jungian approach, but are inherently aware of its value. While almost all initially demur from taking it on, they do come along and the levels of fantasy, symbol, and unconscious tapped by this work is great indeed. Much of the needed analysis can be done this way. Many of them then go on and use these techniques in their own therapeutic work.

Thus far we have omitted the mention of a group therapeutic approach with such patients. While almost all of them have taken part in at least one encounter group, or in more formalized group therapy, we find that coordinate group work with individual therapy can help considerably. Again, the therapist-patient resists the idea, but it is made more palatable for him in that we remain the group leader, and all of the group members are therapists themselves. The continuity of his ego and his treatment is maintained. Again, such group work is short-term and not a part of every therapist-patient's treatment.

It seems fitting that therapists themselves should benefit from the discoveries of Freud on an equal basis with their patients when such techniques can be helpful to them. Some of the difficulties involved in doing this have been described. In every possible sense, the therapist who becomes a fellow sufferer profits by it on both a growth and self-development basis, but the situation is certainly uncomfortable for him. The less the imposed gap between him and his patients the easier it becomes for him.

---

[7] Burton, A. *Interpersonal Psychotherapy. Op. Cit.*

94

Part II

PRIMARILY ON THE PATIENT

CHAPTER VIII

The Fully-Analyzed Patient

BY CONSENSUS, one of the most ambivalent areas of the practice of psychoanalysis and psychoanalytic psychotherapy are the final goals of treatment. No psychotherapist seems to be able to say definitively when a psychotherapy should stop—when the promise of humanity through psychic intervention has been fulfilled. People returning for refreshers to psychotherapy are becoming so frequent that the end-point of the process is now in this way being called into question. In related areas, one of the deeper and less known aspects of general medicine is the fact that many patients do come on and off for treatment for their lifetime and, furthermore, that physicians unconsciously encourage such a longitudinal health style. One has only to consult the case files in dermatology, allergy, internal medicine and similar medical specialties to see that this is so. Psychotherapy, on the other hand, proclaims as one of its maxims that the patient should not come for consultation one moment more than he needs to, and governs itself strictly according to the principles of parsimony. It in fact lives in dread of interminable analysis. It may perhaps be that the refractoriness of mental problems, and the indigenous

97

resistance of patients to the cure, obtrude upon the need for parsimony. But, it is interesting to note, few statistics are available as to just how long patients do persist in psychotherapy, how many need later to return, and how many even clandestinely seek a second or third therapist in their lifetime after the primary treatment has been completed. Burton[1] reports from other sources the remarkable case of a woman who has been in analysis for 21 years with three highly reputable psychoanalysts and is apparently still not cured.

Final states of existence arrived at through treatment procedures require proper linguistic notations as well as indigenous symbolizations to characterize them. Thus a study of the literature revealed that whatever the endpoints of psychotherapy are they are denoted by a whole host of charismatic or metapsychological terms, all of which are furthermore defended by vested interests of one or another scholar or school of psychotherapy. This evolved list from the literature is given below, but cannot in any sense be said to be definitive. It is true that other investigators might come up with a somewhat different list, but their conceptual essence is well stated and illustrates the thesis offered here.

LIST OF END-POINT GOALS IN PSYCHOTHERAPY

1. Authenticated
2. Choosing (and responsible)
3. Disclosed
4. Freed-up
5. Fully-analyzed
6. Fully-functioning
7. Genital
8. Happy
9. Healthy
10. Individuated
11. Insightful
12. Integrated
13. Loving
14. Mature
15. Normal
16. Self-actualized
17. Self-affirmed
18. Self-fulfilled
19. Self-realized
20. Wider consciousness

To test the limits of the use of such end-point metaphors, we sent a questionnaire to 25 psychoanalysts and psychoanalytic psychotherapists, all of eminent treatment stature,

---

[1] Burton, A. *Interpersonal Psychotherapy, op. cit.*

and all whom had in their published works consistently used one or more of these terms. Eighteen replies were received. We also sent the same questionnaire, necessarily modified, to 25 pastoral counselors in California noted for their counseling practices and, in addition, personally interviewed most of the 20 who replied. A second control phase of the study involved open-ended interviews with full-time practicing bartenders who for the purpose of this study were conceived of as psychotherapists of a special social kind. The questionnaire used with the psychotherapists and ministers was as follows:

QUESTIONNAIRE

I. The end-point of a psychotherapeutic experience is frequently a varied if not nebulous thing. When is a person fully analyzed or treated? Assuming that you participate in setting individual therapeutic goals, what do you opt for in your clients both practically and idealistically? Do your clients tend to break off before the maximal goal of realization is reached? Do you tend to settle for more and they for less?

II. The following terms have all been used to describe the optimal state of human functioning. Do you consistently prefer one over another? Is there some historical, experiential, or empirical reason for your choice? Do you consider these terms interchangeable and would you agree to the standardization of a single one of them?[1]

a. Self-actualized	h. Integrated
b. Authenticated	i. Satori
c. Self-realized	j. Loving
d. Self-fulfilled	k. Happy
e. Individuated	l. Self-affirmed
f. Nirvana	m. Normal
g. Freed-up	

III. What is the peak of human functioning? What is the fulfillment toward which all men should strive? Please describe what this has involved as you have seen it through your own sufferings and joys.

---

[1] The list grew somewhat after the questionnaire had been sent out.

IV. Can you recall a person you have worked with, individually or in a group, who attained fulfillment? Would you please describe his fulfillment here in considerable detail?

V. Have you found that people, once fulfilled, stay fulfilled, or that they need to reinforce their fulfillment by new therapeutic or other experiences?

VI. As a psychotherapist, how have you gone about fulfilliig yourself? Please spell this out in some detail in the best way possible.

VII. Do you believe that consciousness-expanding drugs can be useful in finding fulfillment?

VIII. It has been said that the existential thrust toward fulfillment may itself be a neurotic drive, since the human condition is realistically one of despair. Do you preconsciously urge your clients to "make the best of it," or do you offer them the opportunity of "beating their heads against an impenetrable wall," in the hope that something may someday eventually happen?

It is not the purpose of this study to discuss the particularistic findings of the questionnaires, but rather to use them as a backdrop for certain generalizations in regard to endpoint metaphors. For example, none of the respondents were happy with the end-point metaphors, but none wanted them completely interred, and only a rare few would agree on the standardization of a single one of them. They in addition showed unease with the entire concept of our research and long—or extremely short—disquisitions on the items were returned: some with eloquence and some with acerbity. Thus, to illustrate the styles of response, the reply of two psychotherapists to query I: "When is a person fully analyzed or treated?" are given. Respondent I says:

> Never! Life is a continuously problem-solving process at various points in which a person may need help. He should receive it then as briefly, and efficiently, as possible.

Respondent II puts it this way:

> I actively participate in the discussion of therapeutic

goals with 'patients' all along the line. Primarily my impact comes from an honest presentation of my own life goals, my sense of values and my preferences as to the timing of when I can realistically expect to achieve this or that milestone.

In my participation regarding goals, I leave much room for the "patient" living his own life in a way very different from mine. *I present my own ideals as information, not as recommendations.* Here are some of my goals:

1. An agreement with myself as to when I may be *spontaneous, impulsive,* and *seek immediate satisfaction.* At the same time, to agree with myself in regard to satisfaction which can be achieved only in the course of prolonged living efforts. For example, when meeting people in my own home I may impulsively hug someone whom I know with affection, but would not do so in a public situation with the same person. In terms of long-range satisfaction, I would allow 10 or 15 years to achieve a "good marriage" because I don't know how to get there any quicker. Whenever possible within socially acceptable limits I seek satisfaction in the immediate present, while always allowing time for growth in matters where this cannot be helped in order to get what I want.

2. *Making more money* or somehow managing to be more affluent financially seems to be the natural concomitant of any successful therapeutic effort.

3. A gradually *decreasing inclination to fight against social restrictions* (so that a person is not hindered by such things as getting locked up in jail) is to me a sign of adult maturing. When a 'patient' continues making major trouble for himself in society this would suggest that somehow something went wrong during the therapeutic effort.

4. *Radiant physical health* is a significant symptom to me of emotional health. My 'patients' almost routinely improve in their physical well-being when their growth effort goes well, so I have come to take this almost for granted.

---

3 All italics in the quotation belong to the original author.

5. *A special kind of selfishness* is to me characteristic of human maturity. The grown up person freely gives of himself when he has a full hand with which to give, and seems necessary for his personal welfare in the existential present and also in the long run. For example, I see a mature person forgiving his parents for selfish reasons in regard to any grievances he may have from childhood or later, and honoring them with as much affection as possible without thereby letting them dominate his life.

6. The most satisfying experiences of my emotional growth are an increasing capacity and *readiness to freely love others* as I have opportunity to know them. The joyful part of this is my sense of being emotionally rich, and to some extent able to arrange opportunities where it's appropriate for me to share my affection. It has seemed important to me that I not somehow ask to be loved back by the other person, even though I hungrily accept it when others give to me.

It is interesting to note that the psychotherapeutic heroes of our time—Freud, Jung, and, say, Carl Rogers—all found it necessary to somehow exploit an end-point metaphor. But Freud perhaps less so than the others. Freud was always the sober realist—even the pessimistic realist—about what analytic treatment could do for anyone. Jung, on the other hand, given to flights of brilliant fancy, stressed his concept of individuation in most of his writings, but held it out as a form of paradisiacal lure to which only a few could aspire after strenuous rites. Rogers, a clinical psychologist (with theological training) , is perhaps the one single person alive most responsible for the metaphors "fully-functioning" and "self-realization," which are by now in the public domain. There seems to be a positive correlation between the therapeutic promise offered patients in this way and the formal training received by the psychotherapist. Those trained in medicine tend to promise little and do their best to attain whatever that little is. Those trained in the social and behavioral sciences promise more but deliver less than promised. Those of theological persuasion offer the highest point of personal

102

metapsychology but, it seems to us, fail to deliver, except perhaps in terms of indigenous faith dynamics. At any rate, the openness and uncertainty of the healing structure calls for an ideological principle which overrides the techniques available to that structure as a way of perhaps compensating for its inadequacies. Otherwise, the cure might never go forth! Encounter group facilitators, for example, pride themselves on their passive non-intervention in the goals of their clients; but by their derived public image, their public demonstrations, and their written works, they promise more end-point metaphors than anyone else. Such healers decry the narrow goals of psychotherapy and offer to broaden them particularly on the level of consciousness and in regard to the body.

It must be apparent that few people would undertake a long-term psychotherapy if there were not a "promised land" somewhere in the offing. This of course assumes that their suffering is socially manageable and that they have a choice about what they do about it. Patients today not only bring neurotic symptoms to the consultation room, but they suffer as well from the "unused life." The neurotic symptom is often only the most flagrant sign of this. And the vast numbers of non-diseased persons, some also patrons of psychotherapists, but who principally have the problems of boredom and alienation, what has been called the existential neurosis, also seek desperately for the same end-point of fulfillment. The entire drug scene is in a sense given over to finding it as well. Can we perhaps conclude that the tension/conflict theory of psychoanalysis is being replaced by a fulfillment/ nirvana theory?

Thus it is not usually enough today to dispel inhibiting and obstructive symptoms—phobias, obsessions, compulsions, anxieties, guilt, etc.—but a new or revised state of being has to be offered the patient. Behavioral re-conditioning, hypnotic and relaxation techniques can suitably modify such symptoms, but invariably the patient either develops secret substitutions or wants a greater state of fulfillment than he gets with reduced anxiety. This was at any rate always implicit in our work; but today the patient not only demands something more but assesses himself continuously for it. One can therefore see why our respondents were so loath practically to give up their end-point metaphors.

In a certain sense, psychotherapists have analogically to offer their patients an implicit freedom or fulfillment comparable to the pastoral counselor who may employ concepts of heaven and godhead as his mode of intervention. But in the psychiatric model, it is not "good works" which provides the state of "grace" but a historical process of scientific self-mortification which chafes but changes things. Psychotherapists sometimes have to deceive themselves in this area for our appreciation of ourselves as "objective scientists" is often our most prominent ego asset, and we do not easily yield it. But a certain momentary detachment reveals that within this learned objectivity, and almost parallel to it, lies a creative force which has as its moral base the need to make things better for people. The world's most benevolent group of men—and psychotherapists are certainly included here—see humanity as belonging not to the tormenting clutches of Hieronymous Bosch or Goya, but within the sweet heavenly settings of the Tiepolos.

If one looks at the products of psychotherapy, or even at the fully-analyzed healers themselves, then self-fulfillment, or whatever we call it, seems more a rarity than a fact. Most patients are dissatisfied with the outcomes of long-term psychotherapy, even when it is successful by our usual standards. But one rare respondent finds that a number of his patients have indeed found fulfillment. He describes it as follows:

Yes, several of my clients have attained fulfillment. One male of 30, for example, had never been able to make it with females; was an arrant procrastinator; was terribly anxious most of the time; and was often depressed and near suicidal. I saw him for a total of two years, mainly in group therapy. Now he has finished his work at medical school, is a very busy and absorbed practitioner, has warm relations with many of his patients and several of his ex-girlfriends, imperturbably speaks his mind about many things no matter what people think of him, is happily married, is unusually open and unhostile, and will almost certainly remain uncatastrophizing no matter what sorry events may occur in his future life. He constantly keeps "growing" and has a vibrant attitude toward himself, his close associates, and toward life.

At any rate, psychotherapists are solvers of their own unconscious problems as well as those of their patients. Psychotherapy is in a crude sense a vocation for the unique; the patient is of course the most unique of all; but the psychotherapist, it must be said, has basically ritualized his anxiety and despair and somehow turned it into social service and reward. But despair is a proper basis for empathy and it requires no apologetics. What is disturbing, however, is that man *qua* scientist offers the patient a "heavenly star," a mythology, an evanescent metaphor, all in the name of self-knowledge and reality. Freud would not have approved of arriving at a proper goal through an incorrect means. We say to the patient, "Have faith in me and my wonderful process and you will be fulfilled," and we even offer ourselves as a model of that specific fulfillment. The truth, however, seems to be that psychotherapy is as yet a most limited set of procedures, abjured by the vast majority of the world's people, and any improvement whatsoever in existence or behavior through its means is to be humbly and gratefully received. Is it possible to be realistic in this way with a patient without scaring him away from the process, or without offering him end-point metaphors which are ideals and not realities—and possibly never even realizable? Humanism in social science calls for the widest possible behavioral arena for man, and certainly not confining him by a construct objectivity which is not yet the proven ultimate reality. A psychological science without symbol, icon, or myth would at this point be so stark as to approach a surgery which flourishes only by removing the offending organ.

In the total history of man, the movements most significant for man's social evolvement have not been of the scientific variety. Science was at any rate a late comer to the social scene. It was the philosophico-religious ideas which have moved mountains in the past and, alas, sometimes the mountain was moved to the wrong place, or the wrong mountain was displaced. Medicine has not really changed that much since Galen or Maimonides, but the philosophy of existence and culture has. To keep men living together, to keep them from being submerged by the hardships of life, to keep aggression and war circumscribed, and similar hardships, may call for heavenly promises. The faith in a God is the belief of a better state of being to come. And the fact that man succumbs so readily and easily to such constructs is proof of his need for them. Psychotherapy is not *pari passu* immune to this. The proscription of end-point metaphors might indeed work a hardship on our patients who after all come to us to be rescued in a way. To do so would perhaps reduce the *hope* aspects of treatment, which is always the important but unheralded element in the treatment anyway. All men, in their deeper recesses, dream of the "eternal return," Eden before the serpent, the Islamic houri, and the Hindu Apsarases. This need is a basic existential fact of psychological life of the 20th century. Whether we agree or disagree with this bit of irrationality, the end-point metaphor may be our unconscious compromise between the needed objectivity and the needed mysticism.

The longer one spends doing psychotherapy the less is one convinced of any final end-point in treatment. We ourselves can no longer seriously countenance any point or peak of final cure. We recognize instead that psychotherapy is never finished and that, furthermore, only death finishes it. There are of course stopping points in the life course, periods of maximization of function, and this is what we mean when we talk about goals. The final goal is perhaps a philosophic issue rather than a psychological one. Most people in the world never begin a psychotherapy; a few never end it. What makes for the differentiation, we do not know. But psychotherapy serves humanity well in periods of unusual stress and in periods of truly creative evolvement. It also serves for some of us to keep the omnipresent wolf of psychosis away from the door. Psychotherapy comes to the scene when a major creative change of life order has been incubated, but the creative vehicles Eros, Agape, and Thanatos are inhibited from realizing it. By the time most people actually come to psychotherapy, they are already committed to the social process which it represents. It is only for them to approve the outer trappings of its structure, and once approved, they are hardly noticed even if years go by in psychotherapy.

This does not mean that psychotherapy is interminable, or should be, but that only the failure to recognize that the "helping hand" can come in many forms and in many ways can make it interminable. Probably the best psychotherapy is the one which allows the incorporated image or symbol of the healing force to go on after the psychotherapy itself has stopped. We might say that the analytic process stops but the analytic attitude continues. Psychotherapy perhaps goes on too long now, and the search for shorter forms are the compelling compensative motif, but this comes about from the failure to define precisely what happens after separation of patient and psychotherapist. We perhaps need to tag patients like salmon and we might be terribly surprised at the findings!

In patients we call schizophrenic, in certain severe neurotics, in many personality disorders, in the existentially disenfranchised and the non-diseased patient, the analytic introject (or attitude) becomes a part of the character structure, that is, its image becomes attached to the damaged nurturant base from which the character structure originally formed. It then goes on to share its elements side by side. There are now, for example, encounter group members for whom living from marathon to marathon is the way of life. Many of the "analytically-imprinted" sooner or later become lay or professional therapists themselves, that is, they merely shift from couch to chair. In these instances there can be no endpoint, for the process instead becomes the cure. There is however a safety factor in possible interminable psychotherapy in that the unconscious sometimes takes over and resists to the point of forcing separation of the participants. While this permits us to point the accusing finger at the patient, there may be a biological protection mechanism in it, and the dynamism should perhaps be respected more than it is. It is interesting to note in reading Freud's letters that some of his favorite and involved analysands left before he was

107

ready, and even his skill, understanding, and charisma were not enough to hold them in psychotherapy.

We suppose that in the long run any psychotherapy frees the patient from the burden of "progress," from the toils of civilization, and effects a return to a more pristine man. Identified patients are simply not great athletes, are not worshippers of nature, or even aesthetically involved with deep beauty, etc. Somewhere along the line the patient missed the message of the natural world. The "idea" supersedes its actional component: neurosis is a life of mental action displaced from the natural world itself. Psychotherapy, regardless of the end-point metaphor, is freedom for the patient from technical and social instrumentation and a reappreciation of the calmness and dignity of natural processes. But this is not the end of therapy but its epiphenomenal accompaniment. Some have even put it that we become less frontal and more limbic.

But what counts in the ego is ontic thrust. There are patients who disregard their symptoms for their work; but still others who disregard their work for their symptoms. Freud wrote that relatively ignored little jewel, *Civilization and Its Discontents*, while his jaw and palate were being eaten away by cancer, and while he was having multiple cutting operations. Aldous Huxley was writing "The Doorway to Perception" on an airplane with us several years ago when he knew he was dying of cancer. Both might justifiably have folded their hands and stayed in bed.

No one has yet described a typology in which the order of persons might be an ontological dyad of the following kind: (1) persons who are forced to compromise ontic thrust by accepting any or all suitable life substitutes; and (2) those who are willing to pay any price rather than accept any such substitute. While much of this choice goes on at an unconscious level, we would submit that the decision is early set down as perhaps part of the reaction to the first negation or hostility encountered in the world. The earliest infant either subsides into a beaten socialization or he copes by thrusting himself deeper and deeper into the ego fire. Aggression is the force of dissidence, but to be valuable it must not destroy

108

either the dissident or the environment from which he dissents. Most long-term patients are by definition Type 2, for their ontic thrust does not permit them to accept the compromise others do; they are aggressive seekers, but they have certainly been seeking in the wrong places. Any psychotherapy which, like a lobotomy or stereotactic surgery, curtails ontic thrust does not really favor the patient even if it leaves him more comfortable. Some of our most gifted artists, say, Rilke, have hesitated to be analyzed for precisely this reason.

There is therefore no fulfillment or realization of self as such, only a life-process with certain markers along the way and for which no obsession with the realization of self is mandated. The truly fulfilled life does not stop to consider its fulfillment. Psychotherapists who themselves ponder such things compulsively are grist for their own treatment mill. To be self-realized is not to seek self-realization but to be it. It is true enough that the patient has difficulty seeing his assets, and has to be helped in this way, but when some "ultimate realization-drive search" replaces the dignity and despair of the general human burden, then a philosophy or a religion is replacing the psychotherapy.

Our ministerial control group apparently has a much easier time of it then we do. If our pastoral counselor is a believer, then his final goals of counseling rest somewhere in the dynamics of faith and the godhead. Counseling problems are handled by routine counseling techniques; but in a severe crisis of counseling, regression to a theological structure is the norm. It is thus difficult for him to be technically rational when an overpowering spiritual "rescue service" waits in the wings. Thus one minister, when asked the query on, "When is a person fully counseled . . . Do you settle for more or less?" said:

> Sometimes I settle for more. That is, in case a person comes in to save his marriage, I feel that the focus may be in the wrong place, that if he doesn't get his way he will quit. I would prefer that he see beyond success or failure of marriage to face the realities of life and become fully human, regardless of the outcome of the marriage issue.

109

Sometimes I settle for less. If they have impossible dreams, and cannot accept their limitations and the limitations of others, then I try to help them see the various options that are open to them.

But in a later question, the same respondent said:

Also it is my experience that God who supplies my love and strength for my work gives freely to me as I become a channel of His concern for others.

It seems that despite the faith in a godhead, of security in established ritual, of the availability of "indulgences" in various forms, the clergy are the greatest purveyors of the end-point metaphor. Could it be that since birth and death are more or less their special professional province, that they become fixated upon, and concerned with, the ultimate experience? All religions have historically promised salvation—only the means of the saving have differed. End-point metaphors go well with salvation—way points to even a higher order of grace—and it becomes easy for the pastoral counselor to offer something-such in life as well as the promise of it after death. And religion has always carefully regulated ecstacy and joy, along with damnation, as falling into its special province. The Judaic and Christian religions have a covert—and not so covert—hostility to Freud, which he of course returned, because he would not allow the myths and metaphors of salvation, and really even the milder end-point metaphors, to be considered at all. He would settle only for the reality and rationality of life as he saw them. Jung, it must be noted in passing, was more open here.

Sixteen full-time career bartenders from a variety of bars in a city of 250,000 people in Central California served as the second control group and were interviewed in depth early in 1970. In an open-ended interview the following queries were all brought up:

1. Why do people come regularly and consistently to the bars?
2. Would these people rather be behind the bar than in front of it?

3. What is the nature of your deepest relationship to any one patron?
4. Do you respect your patrons as a group?
5. What is it they currently and ultimately want out of life?
6. What role does alcohol play in this process?
7. Are there any differences between the men and women who come to you?
8. Do you feel that bars are helpful to your patrons?

The purpose of using bartenders as a control group was to determine whether the bar offers something in the way of fulfillment to a person which psychotherapy does not. People go to bars for many reasons. Some go not because they are alcoholic, or seek male or female pickups, need to consummate a business deal, or allied reason, but because they are lonely, and the bartender, his ambience, and the alcoholic solvent, offer them something meaningful. Bartenders report numerous patrons of this kind, many never have more than two drinks, and the established relationship apparently means something important to the patron. As one bartender said, "They miss me . . . many come by at night just to say goodnight to me."

The bars sampled were all middle-middle, or upper-middle class bars, which cater precisely to those persons from which psychotherapy draws its patients. The bartenders had worked in bars for a minimum of 10 years and were all journeymen.

Summing up the essence of these interviews with the bartenders, the conclusions are as follows. Bar clients seem to seek the same fulfillment as do the clients of psychotherapists, but they rarely go to psychotherapists to find it. They prefer a group approach, with alcohol as a medium, and while they have an important relationship with the bartender, they resist a transference, and he resists them. They place major emphasis on the interpersonal moment, and basically refuse to tamper with their fantasies, structures, and resistances. Bartenders are notoriously ego-tough characters and they do not supply end-point metaphors as do psychotherapists. Their deep regard is minimal, even mildly spurious, but they offer

111

an ear and a certain sympathy. The bar also gives community in a relatively inexpensive and innocuous way heightened by the alcohol.

There is in conclusion to all these musings no apparent solution to the end-point metaphor. One can really never be fully analyzed, fully self-realized, or totally fulfilled, because these are static end-states which, if ever attained, lose their meaning as life vectors and may amount to death. Only the process of finding them has meaning, and whether or not a "pot of gold" is actually at the end of the rainbow may indeed be an irrelevant event. But two ethical conditions surround end-point metaphors and their understanding is necessary and inherent to the practice of psychotherapy. The first is that the psychotherapist himself be aware of the mythical (and mystical) nature of the final growth concepts he seeks; and, second, that the plethora of such conceptions be unified into a somewhat better scientific notation. Before we can do this we however need to study what fulfilled people are, instead of merely idealizing them. Maslow did this to his great credit. In this way we can perhaps make better sense of the goals of psychotherapy. Some fiction in our work may still be necessary, and maybe the best we can hope for at this time is something comparable to the announced goals of Bugental. "To help patients see their lives whole and with as little distortion as possible."[4] The rest may well follow. At any rate, an open consciousness sets limits to end-point metaphors, and the question may resolve itself by the even further extension of the cognitive.

---

[4] Personal communication.

CHAPTER IX

The Interminable Patient

MANY YEARS AGO, when we worked in a state hospital, we had a patient, a man about 50 years of age, in one of our therapy groups. The particular ward in which he was resident consisted of long-term, chronic, burnt-out cases for whom custody rather than therapy was the rule. It was our lot to be assigned this ward, and we were determined to extend the benefits of human encounter to it. We selected him for group therapy for reasons we are now not sure of, but he seemed the most open of a bad prognostic lot. He came faithfully to the sessions, smiled benignly, but never said a thing. When directly spoken to he replied monosyllabically; it was impossible to tell in the 25 hours of group meeting whether or not he had been reached at all.

As it so happened, there came a cyclical upper administrative push to get chronic patients out of the hospital, and Mr. Paraikos, as we will call him, was selected by the ward psychiatrist for discharge. He was single and, as far as we know, had never even had a visitor. The hospital had been his home for more than two decades. He did not seem psychotic, if he had ever been, but was socially dilapidated, as

113

we often find in the long-term cloistered patient. As usual, he made no objection when departure was brought up, and he was set up in a rooming house under auspices of the county welfare department. The plan was that the state employment service would quickly find a job for him.

He had always interested us for even in a milieu in which the abnormal and grotesque were far from unique, he radiated even more psychic pain of a special sort than the others. When we met on the hospital grounds, we always exchanged affable courtesies, and we always wondered about his long sequestered style of life, and the nature of his psychic content.

We lost sight of him after he left. But one day we met him on the streets of the community in which the hospital was located. He seemed even shabbier than usual, plodded along looking for cigarette butts in the gutter, and said that no one wanted to hire him. He was totally without friends or promise, but said he would keep at it, hoping for the best. We gave him a cigar and were rewarded with a shy thanks.

We would from time to time accost him in the same way, and his situation seemed to be becoming worse and worse. After about six months he still had not found a job, and no friends, and his welfare allowance permitted only the barest marginal existence. Finally, in desperation for him, we asked him if he wanted to go back to the hospital, pointing out that he had a certain security there, companionship, and a whole host of medical and ancillary-medical people dedicated to making him comfortable. We said that we would gladly make the arrangements for his return. He politely declined, mumbling something indecipherable, and then shuffled off. Subsequently, we repeated our offer each time we met him, since his circumstances never seemed to improve. He declined our offer each time. By the time we left this particular hospital for a new position about a year later, he was still nondescriptly walking the streets of the city with no change in his status.

Over the years we have thought about him at odd moments. We wondered what it was about his ego that made him persist in being a community member rather than a member of the sick hospital fellowship. Why did he give up the hospital prerogatives which society provides for people with his problem and which are not even available to some of the rest of us? He was well treated there, had the freedom of the grounds, could work or not as he pleased, and could go into town. If he wanted occupational or recreational therapy, and even psychotherapy, they were not beyond the realm of reason. Finally, he had invested 20 years of living in the hospital, and habit and familiarity count for something. It seemed to us that if we could understand his special situation, we might attain an insight into those people we had failed to reach there.

It took five or more years of introspection before we had sufficient closure to be able to relate his condition to what occurs generally to people. It appeared to us that he might be some kind of fictional hero who lived out his fate and suffering in this particular way, and not unlike the heroes of Herman Hesse, Nikos Kazantzakis, William Faulkner, and similar writers. There are apparently some people in the world who never submit to a rational, ordered fate but are propelled by hidden motives into a perpetually quixotic style of life and which we therapists have only the faintest glimmerings of. Their motives go beyond the pleasure principle, beyond money, sex, and power. We were also impressed at this time by patients being seen privately who never seemed to succumb to culture, to reason, to pragmatism, and to their special circumstances but strove almost endlessly in psychotherapy for something evanescent but terribly important to them which never seemed to come. It seemed to us that society might contain two kinds of people: those who submit quickly to its mandates—sublimation, hospitalization, and existential delimitation—and those, like Mr. Paraikos, who rebel against it and never do really throw in the compensative towel until they die.

Freud's discussion of the possibilities of interminable analysis then came to mind and we remembered that we had never really been happy with that famous essay. We had written once that no psychoanalysis or long-term psychotherapy is really ever finished in that the patient carries the therapist around symbolically for the rest of his life, the way

115

one does with a mother. If the transference was indeed a proper one, it is no great exaggeration to say that the therapist in turn has similarly "stored" the patient in his emotional information bank and retrieves him from time to time at odd psychic moments. What then is the nature of the ontic thrust which in some men forces quick cultural capitulation but in others only death ends the personal defiance? Was Mr. Paraikos one of those rare latter birds? There is similarly an analogue here with the truly great creative person whose outlandish discovery is made against—and in the face of—all of the customs of society and for which severe castigation usually follows. Is there a special order of life warrior we have failed to note in the personality of some people, and is it a socially desirable one?

The quietism of psychotherapy has from time to time disturbed us for its message is basically "adjustment"—"make the best of a world you didn't particularly make." Psychotherapy is in a revolutionary sense a "don't rock the boat" philosophy, for if Western culture were to be uprooted by its psychological or youthful dissidents there might no longer be a psychotherapy as such. (It had always seemed to us that society's marginal and humorous tolerance of psychoanalysis was something based upon a poorly balanced hostility in which it made no great social difference whether the therapist was destroyed in the process of the cure.) Ours is a displacement of social activism and rebellion to an inner subjectivism and which can in the long run harm only the subjective person himself. This is of course society's protection, which is said by Szasz to be the healer's covert function as well. It comes out badly in the mental hospital where the patient is usually sacrificed to the common mass weal. But social or group pain is still pain, and it is only now that youth is pitted against age, poor against rich, black against white, urban against rural, etc., that we are forced to countenance the meaning of individual rebellion in the personality. This is something Camus struggled with but never quite solved.

This chapter is an attempt to deal with one facet of the above problem by examining some motives of the "interminable" patient. Inexorable resistances, infantile fixations,

116

insufferable lack of ego capacity, inability to form a transference, persistent dependency, etc., have never satisfied us as the complete story of the "interminable" patient. These it seemed to us, were all negativities; but could there be positive drives in such patients in the direction of ideals, rebellion, and the like which in their own dynamic way were constructve for their life story when viewed from the inside of that life?

All psychotherapists of necessity meet patients in their practice who though cured by available criteria, or maximally helped in their functioning, refuse to give up their therapeutic sessions. Now certainly there is no exact end-point to therapy, or at least no reliable way of assessing when that point has been reached. Freud put it this way: "The business of analysis is to secure the best possible psychological conditions for the functioning of the ego; when this has been done, analysis has accomplished its task."[1] Rogers, in his client-centered approach, left it totally up to the patient to decide when his help was maximal.[2] Between these two polarities a vast difference of opinion exists as to when a psychoanalysis or long-term psychotherapy is finished—and also who decides that it is finished. We have a very few patients in therapy who have received anywhere from 400 to 1,500 hours of treatment, and the disabling symptoms for which they had originally presented themselves have now long abated. By all criteria their treatment should have been terminated. In one case, a hysterical woman became blind and could not cross a busy intersection to get to her work, and she was about to lose her livelihood to which she clung desperately; in a second, a man locked into an unhappy marriage which had no real possibility of succeeding abused all of his energies in the marriage so that he lived a life constantly drained of substance. In a third case, a psychic tachycardia promised lifelong invalidism to a beautiful but unhappy young woman.

In the first example, psychotherapy completely resolved the master defense, so that going to work (or functional

[1] Freud, S. "Analysis Terminable and Interminable," in *Collected Papers* (Vol. 5). New York: Basic Books, Inc., 1959, p. 354.
[2] Rogers, C. *On Becoming a Person*. Boston: Houghton Mifflin Co., 1961.

blindness) was never again a problem; in the second, the patient was able to separate from his wife, commence a divorce action, and find a new love object; in the third, interpretation of the "problem of the heart" permanently abolished the "speeding heart" as a symptom of an interpersonal love deficiency. Of course, some people do come to long-term therapy for more than one major disabling symptom. Thus, the first patient also used obesity as a defense and her weight has fluctuated up and down over the years. The second patient suffered from castration anxiety, which was only in part related to his marriage, and he still has flare-ups of strong passivity feelings which hinder his relationship to women. The third still rejects male masculinity while "living for nothing else." The point is, however, that according to our professional training, all of these patients have met Freud's criteria for maximal improvement. But they refused to accept such decision. They say that they are still deriving help from treatment, want to come to therapy, and continue to pay their fees. In periods of years (rather than therapeutic hours) one patient has been seen for 12 years, the other for seven, and the third for four, all considerable parts of our own professional life.

There are simple administrative solutions to such problems of "interminable analysis" and most therapists employ them consciously or unconsciously. It is possible, on one basis or another, for us to refer the patients to another therapist, trusting that any putative countertransferences or other treatment deficiencies can perhaps be remedied by a new therapeutic personality and a fresh vantage point. In the second instance, it would be possible to frankly admit defeat to the patients by saying that the therapist's goals cannot in this instance be as high as theirs—that this is the best he can do for them; that possibly he lacks the technical ability required for the acquisition of some ultimate life style they are seeking. And finally, one can say to them, that one is tired or bored, and refuse to go on as an unjustified drain on the person of the therapist, and as his prerogative as a professional person.

Now, in actuality, none of those solutions, even though

118

PROPERTY OF WASHINGTON
SCHOOL OF PSYCHIATRY
LIBRARY

commonly practiced, are satisfactory to either the patient or the therapist. If psychotherapy is considered a research laboratory for the understanding of the psyche as well as for the alleviation of distress, then such convenient personal solutions deny to us the hidden mine of knowledge they contain. It is obviously not only necessary to help the patient but to understand how and why we help him. The fact that at considerable cost a patient still wants to see you after you have supposedly "cured" him demands a scientific explanation.

As a non-medical therapist, these long-term non-psychotic patients have from time to time evoked considerable guilt and helplessness in us. We had been taught that protracted therapy invariably arose because of hidden countertransferences in the therapist, say his own dependency needs, or the need to "accumulate" patients or money. But in the "soul" searching we did we were not dissatisfied with the way treatment had been done, with our own person, or with our families or creative life outside of the consulting room. We were genuinely puzzled as to where to look for the "interminable" aspect of the treatment. What caused difficulty was that the patients' persistence in wanting to be with us in such an enduring way tended to arouse hostility and rejection mechanisms in us. We also began to have periods of boredom with some of them which, if boredom persists, is invariably fatal to any treatment. Because of this we finally consulted a psychoanalyst, placing the entire situation, and ourselves, before him.

The conclusions of the consultation were a not-surprising reluctance on his part to advise dismissal of them. He said that if we were a physician we would certainly not withhold digitalis if it was required for cardiac pathology for a remaining lifetime. By this organic analogy, we construed him to be saying that metaneeds were as important as medical ones. We have now come to understand their particular psychic situation, do not glibly remove them administratively, and find it has relevance for generic psychotherapy. This was brought home to us aphoristically by a patient who said, "I cannot stop waiting."

In certain patients, after the phobic, obsessive, compulsive, schizoid, depressive, dissociative, and other neurotic symptoms have abated, a new form of neurosis supplants that which has been worked through. This new neurosis was always part and parcel of the old but was masked by the latter's florid display which, it may be pointed out, justified the patient's claim to illness and handicap. Curing the phobia and the obsession served to expose the new neurotic state of the patient underneath. Now most often patients are happy to have their major impediment—their source of pain and inhibition—removed, and gladly go about the business of their lives without further therapeutic intercession. They know that should additional inhibition occur, the same procedures, and possibly the same therapist, would be available to them. There are, however, those patients who seem constantly to be listening and waiting for something more. They have what I call a Godot Complex[3] in that they are everlastingly waiting for Godot.

As a group, these patients are rational, highly intelligent, well-dressed and beautiful people. Nearly all of them have attained executive or administrative levels in their professions. They reveal a peculiar logical discrepancy between their work lives—in which they are the essence of reality and rationality, making complex industrial and other decisions—and their personal lives which are dominated by the wild fantasies of the Godot Complex. All of them pay a considerable personal and social price for their continuation in treatment, and some are even aware that they are doomed never to find Godot. As a group they were usually religious in pre-adult life, or had religion forced on them, or at any rate lived in a spiritualized home environment. They were made in many ways to feel privileged in childhood by a special loving attention not necessarily given to their siblings. All hated to see infancy and childhood go by and, indeed, they still in essence desire the benefits of their infancy, beyond what we usually see in the neurosis.

---

[3] Beckett, S. *Waiting for Godot*. New York: Grove Press, 1954. We use Godot here as not implying God as Beckett seems to do but of a certain life principle which has escaped them.

The Godot Complex is appropriate for describing these cases because "the Father" in some mysterious way made them a covenant about their existence. This is a metaphorical statement which covers a great deal of psychological reality. All of the patients now recall a (repressed) contract either with God or Father in which they were promised a favorite, inside, and sublime position in the world of men. With one female patient, it is being taken to play golf (with her famous father) without any other member of the family—three female siblings—being present; that she would have sole and total possession of him. With the male patient cited above, an agreement that his father would teach him to be a great lover, and "lady's man," which his father was, and that his mother would love him in response to his new capacities. With the second female patient, that her beauty was as Helen's (of Troy), and that her father would perpetually war with the Greeks for her.

These covenants must not be by any means construed as simple fantasies. The analysis of the patient reveals them to have important foundations in fact. There was in each case described here such a contract even though the terms were variously or vaguely spelled out. These are the ways by which parents consciously and preconsciously bribe or blackmail their children into a loving relationship—then renege on the contract after the child grows up as they must. This is also often the way religion analogically secures performance from people. For some cultures, primitive or civilized, the family contract is binding until death and has to be avenged if abridged. Today's schizophrenic family bears testimony to such residuals.

The Godot Complex gives rise to an expectancy neurosis which follows the more classical anxiety neurosis. The phobic, obsessive, and other symptoms are, as we said before, the screen which protects the patient from the pain of his everlasting expectancy which has a poor basis in possibility of fulfillment. The continual yearning without hope is the most anxiety producing of all. The body particularly comes in for its share of screen function in the form of obesity, impotence, headache, and other psychosomatic manifestations. There is such eternal waiting which, once the screen symptoms have been cleared, becomes exceedingly painful to behold. As can be understood, there is a murderous, repressed hostility toward "Father" for denying what has been promised and is rightfully theirs by contract.

In all of this sexual needs and fantasies play a great part, but so does the power of the individual. The denial of the contract is interpreted as removing every vestige of hegemony, so that the patient loses decision and choice. Their lives are perpetually in the hands of someone else—more powerful than they—as indeed "Father" was.

Now all of this can be called a neurosis—or at least the unfinished aspect of a neurosis—because reality is distorted in favor of a "reality now turned to fantasy." You may have a million dollars in Confederate money, all obtained in good faith, but if one counts on it for pleasure, one rapidly approaches a delusion. In consideration of the fact that "Father" has been historically dead these many years, it is wasteful fantasy and even dissociation, to continue to everlastingly present the old contract for payment. But this is precisely what these patients do—in unrelenting fashion.

It is easy to see how the therapist transferentially becomes the "Father" in the expectancy neurosis. He is in every sense the inheritor and guardian of all that is magical in our culture, and it is precisely he whose cultural function it is to "make up for the deficits of the family romance." As the healer of the psyche, he tames the Furies and brings one to fulfillment and realization. But as a profession we have avoided stipulating the magic for fear of possible embarrassment in what it is we do exactly. But it can be seen that the patient with the expectancy neurosis will not be satisfied with a better sublimation, or even freedom from "disease." He wants a fulfilled existence based upon the contract and looks to the therapist to deliver it. He rebels symptomatically —continues to rebel—until the contract is fulfilled. Seen in this way, the matter does not become one of "terminable or interminable" psychoanalysis in a technical sense. Freud's position begs the question and offers an easy way out. It must of course be noted that the physician in internal medicine often has the same enduring treatment quest put to him, and sees chronic patients for a lifetime. But since the "body" instead of the "mind" is his province, he can detach himself more cleanly from the philosophical aspects of interminable treatment as we have outlined.

There is no final therapeutic solution to the expectancy neurosis except to note that it is a serious and grim business. It is extremely easy if mishandled to precipitate the patient into a suicidal attempt or into a succession of further justifying symptoms. One way of dealing with it is first of all to come to terms with ourselves, as we have described above; to recognize that it *is* illness of a kind and not dependency or unresolved transference, and to take a broader existential and philosophical point of view toward the problem. We gradually but firmly dissociate ourselves in the treatment from Godot. We point out that unlike "Father" we have kept every contractual promise we have made, and that we are most empathic with their dilemma. We try to shift the temporal emphasis from the past and future to the present and reinforce the beauty and worthwhileness of life. We reiterate this over and over almost *ad nauseum,* so that the expectancy that we will fulfill their vanished contract is slowly made more real in its impossibility. We laud their persistence and rebellion—their interest in a more perfect life—and we never ask them to submit to less than what they seek.

The patient of course clings to his expectations with even greater tenacity than he does a libido fixation for the central core of his being is involved. Ultimately, the therapy must reach the point in which the patient must make a choice between either giving up the Godot Complex and living in the reality of the present possibilities or accepting suicide (or its equivalent) as a final solution. It is similar to the alcoholic who must reach bottom before he makes the decision to stop drinking.

These patients finally come to verbalize their life choice and make a decision; but it must be said that most of them stop "waiting and listening" only with the greatest reluctance. It is only when Thanatos, with its grim and desperately intimate reality, forces some of them off the pivot of the covenant that they give it up. Until then, we offer the best psychotherapy has to offer them and wait for the resolution of their contractual expectations.

CHAPTER X

The Presentation of the Therapeutic Face

AS ONE GOES UP THE EVOLUTIONARY SCALE, the face[1] becomes more interpersonally significant. Rhesus monkeys have always seemed to us to have identical faces, and it is indeed difficult to distinguish one Rhesus monkey from another. In man, on the other hand, the ego seems often distinctively lodged in the face, and it is the face which primarily attracts and repels. Human encounters always involve facial scanning of some kind, whereas animal identification is more heavily loaded by olfactory and genital examination.

The human face is the one organ most uniformly exposed and open to the world—and its proper (social) presentation is a matter of some moment in human affairs. Many hundreds of millions of dollars are spent annually in grooming, forming, and reshaping it. It is indeed the face which acts as the agent for the total personality and it is the first to fall into love or hate. Most significant bodily intake is through the face and it becomes the model for higher order introjection and incorporation. Its component organs—nose, mouth, teeth,

---

[1] We technically include the head as part of the face for purposes of this paper.

eyes, hair, and ears, etc.—have from time to time each been cited as a primary source of eroticism and fetishism, if not actually the touchstone of the personality itself.[2] The question must thus be raised as to what human life and human personality would be like if we all had identical faces.

It is indeed strange that the psychopathological literature has few references to the face and then only to the faces of the most severely ill. Of course, a number of investigators have made *ad hoc* remarks about the face and some experimental work reveals that the right and left sides have different meanings.[3] Birdwhistell even developed a notational system of facial behavior,[4] but no systematic account of the face's function in psychotherapy seems to be available.

In our own therapeutic experiences we have again and again been impressed with the face as a vehicle of interpretation and a carrier of emotions. Was it not Freud who reported that he could not bear the patients staring at him eight hours a day, and finally developed the couch as a psychoanalytic technique? So much of psychotherapy is non-verbal, and with this we all agree, but it is not the body itself but the face which "talks without talking." Because the face does also talk verbally that we believe we have ignored its non-verbal properties. A patient told us recently that he could only come to his therapeutic interviews when he could show his face to us in a specific way—otherwise he felt the danger was too great. He worries regularly and consistently what his face will do in specific interpersonal situations, and he fears his lack of control of it. A colleague also told us of a patient he had treated who could not remove his hat in therapy because he believed that a part of his face was missing—which it certainly was not. We have also treated several patients with delusions of parts of their head and face missing. The therapeutic task in every case resolved itself into recovering the missing part. Another patient comes regularly with a

[2] One thinks here of Fliess' ideas of the nose in human personality.

[3] Abraham, P. One body, two faces. *Nouv. Rev. franc.*, 1934, *22*, 409-429; 585-614.

[4] Birdwhistell, R. L. *Introduction to Kinesics*. Louisville, Kentucky: University of Louisville Press, 1952.

"frozen stiff face," a tight mask, and he cannot move a muscle of it. When it does infrequently change tonal posture, things go better with him and he is happier. He reports that his spine and penis have the same rigid incapacity of expression.

Psychotherapist and patient are performers, in the sense of one sociologist, even though one comes for help to the other.[5] Performers have to present themselves in a certain way. They have a "back" region and a "front" region, like any who perform on the stage. A tacit agreement is maintained between performer and audience to act as if a given degree of opposition and accord existed between them. Typically, but not always, agreement is stressed and opposition is underplayed.[6] This is what Goffman calls sustaining a situation by tact.

The face of the therapist is crucial in performance or impression management, which is why Greek dramatists employed masks so profusely. Our experiences in encounter groups using masks reveal that the person not only experiences the mask role but exudes feelings to match. Some, however, are made terribly anxious by the masks and must quickly put them aside. "The image that one status grouping is able to maintain in the eyes of an audience of other status groupings will depend upon the performers' capacity to restrict communication contact with the audience."[7] In such restriction the face is central particularly since psychotherapy can be described as a process in which "secrets" are the currency.

Identity and customary modes-of-being are invested as well in the face and defended most vigorously. Touching faces (together) is often a higher act of human confirmation than sexual intercourse and possibly really rarer in human events. We feel through our face rather than our heart for the heart is incapable of the necessary transformation which the face has as its everyday repertory. The face is mine-me—and being faceless is metaphorically the principal symbol of alienation, of being lost, of not belonging.

---

[5] Goffman, E. *The Presentation of Self in Everyday Life.* New York: Doubleday, 1959.

[6] *Ibid.,* p. 238.

[7] *Ibid.,* p. 241.

Leopold Szondi[8] bases a considerable portion of his "fate-analysis" theories upon the transmission properties of the human face. Not only does he conceive of the face as expressive but as the carrier of latent genetic propensities as well as the higher ones. Szondi would say that not only is being-in-love revealed by the face but the tendency to be explosive resides there as well. He makes many analogies to marital selection, which he feels is done to a considerable extent by facial scanning which matches up hidden latencies and needs. (It has in passing seemed to me that the Szondi Test has in America been rejected out of hand because of the resistances we have to the face as non-verbal communication.)

The history of medicine records a diagnostic practice called pathogonomy. This consists of diagnosis of bodily disease by the condition of the facies. A recent researcher[9] reports that heart disease, polyps, adenoids, chronic liver disease, ulcers, tuberculosis and similar medical conditions are uniquely manifested in the face of the victim. The pigment as well as the structure of the face becomes specifically revealing of the underlying pathology. The facies then come also to represent the psychic reaction to the somatic malfunction through a dynamic psychosomatic mechanism.

A medical interne handling his first therapy patient once asked us how he should hold his face. He was truly frightened that he would give something away which should not be revealed to the patient. We were thunderstruck by the query because the face had never occurred to us as a therapeutic problem before. But in fact, what do we tell tyros in psychotherapy about their therapeutic faces? We are certainly apt to encourage them to peruse the patient's face? Numbers of patients maintain or break the therapeutic contract on the basis of their facial reading of the therapist. They are apt to say, "My doctor has a nice or a kind face; or he has a mean face." Facial-tone expression sometimes means more to patients than what the therapist actually says out of his face.

It must be evident at this point that the royal road to

8 Szondi, L. *The Szondi Test.* Bern: Verlag Hans Huber.
9 Farber, E. M. *Stanford M. D.*, 1968-69, *8*, 26-28.

therapeutic growth may be the face and there is such a thing as facial-style as a part of life-style. Contact with the patient is made through the eyes, through the face, and the face is the barometer of the depth and meaningfulness of the feelings the personality has. Even the psychoanalytic transference can be looked upon as facial in that the parental facies is usually projected upon the analyst. The resolution of the transference neurosis is freedom from precisely that facial threat or from a parental over-weaning facial love.

The face has a large panoply of reactions—voluntary as well as involuntary—which range from total involvement to total uninvolvement. It can be blank, vacant or absent—or inviting, passionate, ecstatic. It can weep, be sad, terrorized, suffering, hostile, biting, sleepy, painful, sucking, stiff, and manifest a hundred other states. All of these we learn to read early, assume, and act-out.

To practice psychotherapy successfully it is necessary to be at peace with one's face. If the therapist dislikes his face, or sees an enemy in it, then his total defensive posture in treatment will be exaggerated. Our own face is one which immediately and sometimes embarrassingly reveals itself, and we have come to learn the difficult way that we and our face cannot dissimulate. This has forced us to employ each therapeutic moment in its own right and to be totally open with the patient. The essential difference between what the face says and what the mouth verbally claims is guilt. The face and mouth therefore need unity and integration. The product then becomes honesty.

Because the neurotic wears the mask of dissimulation, the schizophrenic the face of split affect, the psychopath the jovial vacancy, and the aged the exhausted spirit, it is necessary for the therapist to understand the meaning-reality which lies behind the facial stance of each. The face of the infant is inherently pristine—it smiles, howls, or is benign—it just is. Becoming an adult is the corruption of this virginal facial state in the direction of deception. But the mature deception which is finally attained is itself indicative and prognostic, and a quick scanning of a new patient's face sometimes tells us more than a Rorschach. Thus the Socratic injunction "know thyself" also involves knowing your face, and the psychotherapist must to some degree experience and inventory his own face before he becomes a practitioner. Its possibilities are the range of his emotions, and while he cannot always control them, he must indeed be aware of them. The index of his own social relationships is the freedom of his face to be fully and totally expressive. The paintings (and drawings) of El Greco and Goya are to be contrasted in the transport and constraint of the faces of their subjects.

On a more dynamic level the components of the face are significant for understanding the deeper aspects of the patient. There is the man in therapy with us who constantly fondles his nose, the woman who compulsively arranges and disarranges her hair, the man who bares his teeth, the woman who keeps her eyelids at half-mast in sultry expression, and the woman who cried through eight straight sessions. There is also the totally frigid woman who uses her lipstick to accentuate the vaginal properties of her lips, the one whose eye shadow promises the pleasures of the houri, the dangling pendant earrings of the lesbian, and so it goes. Each facial maneuver or facial-style has its repressed counterpart which is a part of the overall personal life-design itself. It thus makes a difference with one of my patients whether she is wearing her hair up or down when she comes to therapy, and we can in this way immediately tell the state of her being. When it is up, she is her momma's dearest friend and rival, a highly successful personnel executive, a frigidly ravishing woman, all business and no nonsense. When it is down, she is the freed-up hippy, pot-smoking, loving, sweet, generous to all, and indifferent to momma. As our work goes on, her hair is now more often down than up—and we watch her hair with avid interest and participation as a kind of barometer. A professor in treatment fixes us perpetually with frozen facies unlike any other patient we have ever seen. He impresses us with his Sisyphusean suffering. As we continue to work together, we find moments in which his facial muscles are not so tense, and some days they permit a true smile. This would be his particular orgasmic response. He waits afraid of it, but desiring it.

130

It would of course be a mistake to use openness and facial confrontation across the board with every patient. The sense of timing necessary for this is the same as for a verbal interpretation, because it *is* an interpretation. "I care," or "I love you," or "I hate you," or "You are wrong," can be said as well without words and can have the same impact on the patient. Words are late arrivers on such scene. The pregnance of silence is facial. We are always interpreting; but what gets interpreted is what counts. The general background of therapy is facial positive regard upon which a specific facial interpretation is made. These must always be sparing, timely, and meaningful.

Face-to-face showdowns with patients are as frequently constructive as they are unconstructive. They are honest confrontations, not necessarily of a voluntary sort, which attack the therapeutic frustrations and roadblocks which leave all participants helpless. A herculean emotional effort, a face-to-face meeting, is suddenly there to clear the way. The faces under such circumstances come closer together, alter their facial style, and evolve into unique expression—first usually hatred and then more loving. We say face-to-face because eyes, ears, nose, etc., cannot evade their sensory functions and dissimulate when put up against other sense organs of their kind. The outcome is always a feeling of cleanliness and of a readiness to tackle something new. A sort of sneezing out!

The neurotic seems incapable of snarling or biting. The schizophrenic definitely so.[10] Is this a function lost in the process of becoming civilized? Or are there specific parental injunctions against it? Biters and snarlers as actor-outers do not need to internalize their aggression or internalize the need to biologically protect themselves. Neurotics indeed need to be taught how to snarl in treatment and to learn that the sky does not cave in because they do. They have to come to know biting as aggression as well as affection. If the therapist is free to snarl when he feels snarly, the patient comes to recognize the genuineness of even this emotion

---

[10] Lowen, A. *The Betrayal of the Body.* New York: Macmillan Co., 1967.

and experiences the release which comes with snarling. He may then feel free to attempt it himself.

Thus the face becomes an important part of what Goffman calls "the presentation of self in everyday life." Possibly it is more accurate to speak of faces since many of us are convinced that we have more than one. But it is clear that the face is an important aspect of self and that we have tended to ignore it in psychotherapy. Of course, the face is never the body, and the face has now become institutionalized as a cultural communicational medium, and the total body much less so. We expect the face to speak universally to mankind but the body only in solitude or in rare moments of intimacy. More than we are aware our fate, Nemesis, is cast as a face, which is why we often become so frantic about it.

Goffman[11] again says:

> In their capacity as performers, individuals will be concerned with maintaining the impression that they are living up to the many standards by which they and their products are judged. Because these standards are so numerous and so pervasive, the individuals who are performers dwell more than we might think in a moral world. But, *qua* performers, individuals are concerned not with the moral issue of realizing these standards, but with the amoral issue of engineering a convincing impression that these standards are being realized. Our activity, then, is largely concerned with moral matters, but as performers we do not have a moral concern with them. As performers we are merchants of morality. Our day is given over to intimate contact with the goods we display and our minds are filled with intimate understandings of them; but it may well be that the more attention we give to these goods, then the more distant we feel from them and from those who are believing enough to buy them. To use a different imagery, the very obligation and profitability of appearing always in a steady moral light, of being a socialized character, forces one to be the sort of person who is practiced in the ways of the stage.

But staging is incompatible with the aims of psychotherapy.

---

[11] *Op. cit.*, p. 251.

132

A conflict between being and presentation therefore develops. The shock of accidentally meeting one's psychoanalyst in the lavatory, as happened to us, is just that his presentation falls off and his true being revealed. The wider the hiatus between presentation and being, the greater the shock value. Whenever we have allowed psychotherapy to become performance rather than ourselves, the patient has suffered for it. The difference between great healers as men and as healers—almost always a disturbing personal experience on meeting them both ways—is that the healer's being is found to be less than the charisma of his presentation.

The face of course plays the major part in presentation, but also in being. Training for psychotherapy should allow for bringing the two closer together. It is precisely because the face cannot always be emotionally presented that it is feared by psychotherapists and thereby becomes a problem. The solution of course is to have nothing to hide—to not present or perform—but such a suggestion is obviously so idealistic and impractical as to be ludicrous. To be man is to have weaknesses, compensations, and secrets. What needs rather to be done is to share the problematic areas of life with the patient and that such approach is effective has been convincingly shown by Mowrer.[12] The patient demands some amount of presentation, some dramaturgy, and without it he would feel cheated. Thus the pomp of modern-day religions has not necessarily reduced the value and efficiency of the confessional. But again, the patient is not always the best determiner of what he needs for otherwise he would not have patient-status. The therapeutic aim then is for the therapist to learn to allow his being to shine forth, the freedom of his face to express itself, to be fully participative, with of course, the due psychotherapeutic caution which befits non-verbal interpretations of some moment. The peak experience is mirrored in the face.

---

[12] Mowrer, O. H. (Tape recording of a counseling session with a University of Illinois coed loaned to me.)

CHAPTER XI

Hope and Psychotherapy

HOPE HAS RECENTLY COME BACK into vogue as a concept in psychopathology. Erikson[1] mentions it in a recent book as part of the newer frontiers of the human psyche; J. D. Frank[2] discusses the part it plays in the psychotherapeutic process; and Melges and Bowlby[3] correlate hope and hopelessness with the various psychopathological conditions. In our own work with schizophrenic patients we had observed that the chronic schizophrenic was perhaps the least hopeful of all patients, and this finding did not exclude the manic-depressive who singularly lives in the darkness during his episodes. Upon further reflection it occurred to us that hope and schizophrenia might be more intimately related than being simply the effect of a long drawn-out and wearing-down mental process based in regression. For example, in my experience, the mothers of schizophrenic patients would have to be cat-

---

[1] Erikson, E. H. *Insight and Responsibility*. New York: Norton and Co., 1964.

[2] Frank, J. D. The role of hope in psychotherapy. *Int. J. of Psychiat.*, 1968, 5, 383-395.

[3] Melges, F. T. and J. Bowlby. Types of hopelessness in psychopathological process. *Arch. Gen. Psychiat.*, 1969, 6, 690-699.

egorized as hope-less rather than hope-ful people, for they seem generally a concrete, low-feeling, and pessimistic-bound group. If generally true, what part would such maternal life attitudes play in the general hope-lessness which forms in schizophrenic patients, and is even visible in them in the nursery school?

One of the significant functions of the ego is to provide hope. We define hope as a state of being in which a heightened expectancy overrides the objective possibilities of the moment. Hope abridges the probability of an event by the expectation of a greater return than the probability would indicate. Only a small amount of hope is perfectly correlated with reality, that is, that one hopes for what is directly possible. But it should also be noted that hope may sometimes change the probability of the event occurring. The basic fatalism of all biological structure, and what on a philosophical level comes to be called "the human condition," calls for an abridgment of the hardships of life so that man might not fall into a constant pessimism and in this way inhibit his survival. Homo sapiens, given a highly evolved consciousness, and one specifically denied to other species, then required a metaconstruct to accompany it to reduce the acuteness of that particular consciousness. It is perhaps the price he has to pay for being fully human.

Western science has had little place for hope in its conceptual resources; but it should be noted that this hasn't prevented the scientist from personally hoping that his experiments turn out! Hope, and her half-brother, faith, assumed an unwarranted grandiosity under theological and clerical auspices, so that a natural repugnance sets in which resulted in largely shelving the phenomena by the logical positivists. Hope and faith became the *deus ex machina* of the theologian and, by counterreaction, the *bete noir* of the objective specialist. But anyone who treats mental disease cannot help but be impressed by the workings of hope. It is thus the purpose of this chapter to attempt to put the concept of hope into a more proper perspective, at least as far as what we call psychotherapy is concerned.

What makes a man sentenced to a life term (without possibility of parole) hopeful that he will get out; what makes a terminal cancer patient feel that he will finally be saved; why did the inmates of the Auschwitz concentration camp uniformly believe that they would be spared from the ovens? In all of these situations there is objectively no real room for hope. Is hope then merely an illusion—perhaps even a delusion—and is it essentially a magical flight from reality to avoid pain and suffering? If this is so, should man be counseled to give up illusory hope, or to hope less? In psychotherapy we see people whom we know, as scientists, that they have almost no chance of becoming fulfilled. Their character armor is such that the parameters of freedom/growth have become congealed by perhaps something analogous to an imprinting process, and a hardening that leaves very little scope for a verbal relationship process to bring some form of nirvana to them. Should this be revealed? And should they give up trying to become fulfilled when their self-chances are indeed so slim? Should they be counseled to make the best of an imperfect self in an imperfect world?

Psychotherapists as a class are a group of hopeful people or they could not long persist in their profession. They are fully aware, for example, of the "outside chance" in the most determined of human events; of the fact that science does not yet have perfect predictability; and that no one can play an absolute God to anyone else. They have repeatedly seen extraordinary examples of the possibilities of "becoming," which hope provides, mobilizing and energizing what would otherwise be a static or regressive situation. Only people without hope are the truly condemned. Psychotherapy, whatever it is, is certainly hope applied to the self-perception of being hope-less. Therapists are people who everlastingly joust with the impossible—with the hope that the long personality shot will pay off—and while they try diagnostically and in other ways to cast the odds in their favor, the grand payoffs are by contrast few and far between. Yet, psychotherapy is a flourishing entity, and in a sense it is the one area of all of medicine to which hope is delegated.

Death is the final loss of hope. What, of course, man hopes for—the prototype of all his hoping—is that he will gain immunity to death. More hope unfortunately surrounds this aspect of man than any other, and such hope for freedom from death must of course come to a sad resolution. But it makes a difference how man accepts his death. One ever-present problem in today's society is the loss of the hero, that person willing to die gloriously for an overriding social purpose. Another is the fact that death has become mass and meaningless.

This, however, is not exactly the problem of the psychology of hope as we see it. It is instead that the hope of the day must allow facing that daily intrinsic quality of death by producing a life more aware and acute while it still goes on. Hope transcends the drag of finiteness by energizing life projects which would never ordinarily be undertaken to begin with. Hope is the prime ingredient of personal motivation, and hope-ful people have more positive feelings than hope-less ones. All significant creative breakthroughs have originally occurred unrealistically on the basis of hope, and such materializations have happened at least often enough to have changed humanity and the world.[4]

Hope is the projection of the present into the future and is the bridge between reality and magic. Hope occurs on many levels, in many complex matrices, but in schizophrenia it fails because it is merely magical. Hope itself has a grid of probabilities; but hope mostly applies when the probability of the future event is unknowable, undesirable, or unthinkable. A scientist may hope to become a Nobel Laureate, and while the probability in psychology may be almost nil, the fact that he hopes for it adds creative productions to his bibliography and to the world. Hope fluctuates with deprivation and with success, and is an important aspect of esteem and creative work. All intelligence operates within a structure of hope.

Thanatos regularly pulls against Eros, but hope is the mitigating agent of the latter. Love would mostly sink into a morass without hope because its realities are just too tawdry for our romantic natures. A transcending factor is needed

---

[4] Watson, J. D. *The Double Helix*. New York: Atheneum, 1968, for example.

137

in human events, we call it hope, and it serves not only to reduce the repressions of life to begin with, but to displace or ameliorate them once they are fixed. Hope and Eros keep Thanatos at bay and even, in yet unknown ways, psychosomatically influence biological processes.

The mental hospital is a significant personal organization because not only is it the final refuge of the hope-less but it is staffed by large numbers of people who often lack hope as well. My experience has been that a majority of such staff —from psychiatrists, psychologists, social workers, to ward attendants—do not really in their inner being believe that mental illness is curable. They go through certain rituals, which of course help, but do not offer solid hope. The directive emphasis in mental institutions on organic and technical approaches is not so much a matter of having too many patients to treat as an inner disbelief in the nature of the "talking cure" or in the effectiveness of the psyche in healing itself. Mental hospitals attract those who cling to hereditary, organic, structural and similar hope-less theories.

There is a relationship between hope and laughter. Hopeful people laugh more than hope-less ones. The comic can only take place within a projection of a future event. The paradox of outcome, which is the humorous event itself, is a hopeful projection, but with of course an unlooked for concluding twist. One laughs because one is in it; but more so because the laughing situation is itself a hopefully trancending one. Comics seem to live unusually long lives—Jack Benny, Bob Hope, Milton Berle, George Jessel, etc.,—and while hope does not provide longevity, the correlation is an interesting one. The gerontological advice about the future might be to "keep laughing!"

Hope is also coupled with temporality. Closed-time systems have little hope in them because they do not provide for much futurity. Hope takes place only in time, which is maybe why aging leads uniformly to reduced hope. In every individual there is in him a balanced relationship between his past, present, and future. Preternaturally backward-looking people are not unusually hopeful men; those who live merely for the present—say, psychopaths—also have little use for hope; those who live in the future by means of conceptions of karma, heaven, or reincarnation are, on the other hand, only magically hopeful.Fulfillment and identity require a properly weighted matrix of past, present, and future, with hope providing the necessary futuristic balance wheel between the drag of the past and the vicissitudes of the present. Time, the neurosis, militates against hope; but freedom-in-time promotes it.

The ability to make things come true, or to attempt to make things come true, is the basal aspect of all motivational force. Maintaining a goal in the face of its impossibility is salubrious; but after a certain point it becomes absurd. But this is always a personalistic and not a collective determination because there is the everpresent possibility that fiction may turn into reality. Of course, this only rarely happens. But the fact that it does changes the structure of things. Science fiction writers are now in great demand by sober and profit-minded industry because of their earlier prevision.

If a typology of hope-ful and hope-less people were for theoretical purposes established, then schizophrenics and manic-depressives would most certainly populate the latter bin. There is an essential difference, however, between the two diseases insofar as hope is concerned. The manic-depressive crests on the wave of his ambitions, becomes angry or hurt with less than perfection, loves himself deeply in a most concealed way, and his hope fluctuates like a barometer with his implicit or actual achievements. In his best moments, he is an innovative creator who transcends his existence by his works; at his worst, he feels guilty because unfulfilled, often wants to die, and feels totally without hope or promise of redemption.

In the schizophrenic, the matter is somewhat different. The schizophrenic has never had a baseline of hope or achievement, and his schizophrenia can be called "crushed hope." His development has been one psychological failure after another. The pathogen which maternal double-binding represents is not inconsistency in or negation of message but rather that, in a certain abundance, the message quashes all hope of a fulfilled or free existence. Apathy is a state peculiar

139

to and diagnostic of schizophrenia and what it is basically is the fear, the danger, and impossibility of opting for change—for full human growth. Mothers of this kind make the best unconscious jailers of all for they deprive in the name of care and benevolence. Beginning in early childhood, maybe even on the first day, the message sent is: "you are hope-less; your hope exists only in me; and you are forever disappointing me." But we have already said that schizophrenogenic mothers themselves are not known for their high titre of hope. They in fact pass a certain pessimism on to their offspring, compound it, and suppress all attempts to relieve it, even when their child is in psychotherapy. They are anti-hope.

The systematic removal of hope from prisoners of war by brainwashing technique is now fully documented as political and military phenomena and has been shown to be effective in changing personality. This is particularly true where a weakness of the ego exists.

Lost hope brings disillusionment which in some people is the desire to remain disappointed.[5] Schizophrenics act as though success were a catastrophe, or rather their perpetual disappointment in things as they are gives them no basis for replaced object libido. They seem to avoid mourning and restitution at any cost and because the ego is not capable of esteem, they do not become depressed. But disillusionment, which is different from depression, becomes the style but in a withdrawn and affectless way. They then work hard to maintain the disillusionment. Obviously the infantile irregularity in the ability to cathect reduces hope to a self-event which, because it merely involves the self as autism, cannot attain the hope which is always qualitatively interpersonal.

Beyond this, the early pioneers of psychiatry added their bit to the pessimism of schizophrenia. Even the most sanguine of European psychoanalysts threw up their hands at hope for schizophrenia for they considered it an insidious, malevolent, and regressive form of organic disease with only one

---

5 Socarides, C. W. On disillusionment: the desire to remain disappointed. *Br. J. Med. Psychol.*, 1971, *44*, 35-44.

possible outcome. In our own dialogue experience, even such therapeutically optimistic people as C. G. Jung, Manfred Bleuler, and Viktor Frankl subscribe or subscribed to this attitude, and, of course, Freud's ideas about the narcissistic neuroses are now notorious.

The schizophrenic who consulted a healer, or the patient hospitalized in a special milieu set up for him, had his feelings of minimal self-worth regularly confirmed by the "wise old men," the men society places in charge of psychic disease. His surrogate mother, i.e., the doctor, and the one to whom he had unconsciously fled for relief, and who above all should have offered him hope, deprived him further of it, helped drive him even deeper into autism and magic. In a paradoxical way he even closed the access to the hopeful outside. The difference in a diagnosis of manic-depressive disease and schizophrenia is precisely that one has hope and the other does not. Every institution both subtly and unconsciously proceeds to implement the fate of its diagnoses for to do otherwise is to create a split in its own integrity.

Psychotherapists of schizophrenia working within institutonal confines invariably run up against top administration on this point. Hope creates disorder. In the ordered system of the hospital dis-order cannot be tolerated, is seen as inimical to treatment, and most psychotherapy with chronic schizophrenic patients is discouraged. One must then battle not only the patient for his own health but the medical superintendent as well. Only those staff members with the greatest force of hope survive in this conflict.

The postulation of Von Domarus[6] that schizophrenics confuse subject and predicate can be interpreted to mean that since the schizophrenic's future has vanished entirely why have a predicate at all. A predicate in the final analysis is an action. The "I," to complete an act, to have a predicate, must have hope of some kind, some warmth or feeling of an outcome, or why bother with another assured failure. The clinical evidence is that under certain—and often rapid—cir-

---

6 Von Domarus, E. "The Specific Laws of Logic in Schizophrenia," in J. S. Kasanin (ed.), *Language and Thought in Schizophrenia*. Berkeley: Univ. of California Press, 1944.

cumstances some schizophrenics combine subject with predicate beautifully for the moment. Invariably these turn out to be interpersonal situations which offer some hope to the closed and hope-less patient. The break in subject and predicate is not therefore a permanent or irreversible one but can be changed by making action more hopeful.

Schizophrenic patients have at times been called the "walking dead." The allusion to death in relationship to schizophrenia is not a wasted one. We have elsewhere described the schizophrenic as a person who has neither being nor non-being.[7] Schizophrenics cannot live, but neither can they die. They clog the mental hospital with their longevity. In order to live, the possibilities of death have to be visible. The most excruciating and livable existence of all is when one takes risks with one's life, as in battle or in racing at Le Mans. But what happens when the data of finiteness are simply confusion, and the Eros/Thanatos tension does not make any contribution to awareness and existence? Reality is then apt to be deprived of its phenomenological tension and this helps explain the great indifference of the schizophrenic patient. We never before could understand the dilapidation of the chronic schizophrenic in the state hospital until we realized that without the Eros/Thanatos dialogue there is nothing that can maintain psychic systems in force. Nihilism slowly overcomes the momentary small acts of faith by which the human entity is kept operative. And, indeed, the psychotherapy of schizophrenia ultimately leads the patient to a choice of real life or real death. Either one is in a sense a successful resolution of the treatment.

In these terms there is not so much a technique of psychotherapy with schizophrenic patients as a method of instilling hope in them. It is an interesting coincidence that the recognized healers of schizophrenia—say, Frieda Fromm-Reichmann and Marguerite Sechehaye—were also humanitarians of the first order. They radiated confidence, courage and hope not only in treatment but outside of it as well. They were

---

[7] Burton, A. *Modern Humanistic Psychotherapy. Op. Cit.*

142

persons in their own right. In this sense all therapists may require a sufficient titre of hope-induction potentiality before *any* technique they adopt may work at all. That form of communication without words may be the crucial aspect of therapeutic work and hope would certainly be one of the more important ones.

CHAPTER XII

The Therapy of a Non-Diseased Person

THE QUESTION OF TREATMENT for a normal or non-diseased person cannot by definition arise in medicine. Medicine is that aspect of science which mitigates disorder or dysfunction, and to treat, let us say, a normal liver would be a violation of all those canons by which medicine itself became an accepted scientific discipline.

In psychiatry, the aspect of medicine given over to the treatment of mental disorder, the above situation still holds, but a qualification creeps in. While psychiatry attempts to establish the "sick" entity in traditional medical ways, it is not always certain that such a model fits with any great precision. Psychiatry now quite often deals with social illness, which masquerades as mental illness, and many sociologists,[1] anthropologists, and even psychiatrists[2] are challenging the traditional conception of mental illness. In treatment which is family oriented, for example, the "identified" (or "committed") patient does not always turn out to be the "real"

---

[1] Goffman, E. *Asylums. Essays on the Social Situation of Mental Patients and Other Inmates.* Chicago: Aldine Publ. Co., 1962.

[2] Szasz, T. *The Myth of Mental Illness.* New York: Harper and Row, 1961.

patient—and shifts in patient status quite commonly occur during family therapy. Patients committed to mental hospitals sometimes attain patient status because they represent the fulcrum of familial or societal forces rather than being medically sick as such. On the level of personality organization and disorganization, the medical model loses its diagnostic sharpness, possibly because the most useful tools of physical medicine—the X-ray, the analysis of secretions and tissues, encephalography, and such—are only of minor and ancillary value in psychiatry. There are few personality handbooks comparable to the legion of medical ones which give tables of normative limits for various organic functions. In the absence of personality or behavioral norms, each therapist more or less becomes his own norm, and he may not always be fully conscious of the fact that *he* personally represents the norm.

The recognition of this state of affairs has led to increasing attempts to study normal or non-diseased groups of people as a baseline not only for diagnosis but for treatment.[3,4] The inherent scientific error in generalizing from pathological cases only without any form of normative control is now so well known as to not warrant repetition here. What is, however, not so numinous is the fact that pathology (diagnostically) seeks out pathology—that the aspect of science which has pathology as its function tends to find pathology wherever it looks. Pathological sciences cannot seriously countenance the normal, average or non-diseased for their function is to define disablement and impairment and this is what is referred to them. Very few Rorschach tests are in this sense ever labeled normal. There is no adequate image, not only of the personality properties of being normal or non-diseased person, but of the *ideal* person; that is, the becoming possibilities of the human being in his more glorified and non-diseased moments.

---

[3] Maslow, A. H. *Toward a Psychology of Being.* New Jersey: D. Van Nostrand Company, 1962.

[4] Rogers, C. R. "The Actualizing Tendency in Relation to 'Motives' and Consciousness," in *Nebraska Symposium on Motivation,* 1963; The process equation of psychotherapy. *Am. J. Psychother.,* 1961, *15,* 27-45. Also, personal discussion.

Most people dislike considering themselves average—even though most people are average—and when they get ready to die, they usually evaluate their contribution to humanity by a rare and occasional supra-average experience which may have once occurred to them. It is thus not enough at this point to have an intact liver or even an intact ego. The human cortex—unlike in lower orders—makes meaning in life possible, and every organ of a man may be healthy and the person still sick if such "meaning" is absent. Where microscopes, X-rays, and other laboratory equipment are determinatively impossible, disease or non-disease may become a matter of forensics, as it so often does in the case of the plea, "not guilty by reason of insanity." Such forensic differences of scientific opinion occur precisely because X-ray or microscopic analysis of the ego is out of the question.

When we come to the form of healing known as psychotherapy, we are in deeper trouble still. Not only have we failed to define adequately the parameters of what psychotherapy is—its necessary dimensions—but we are not quite certain of the persons best treated by it. Each therapeutic patient has more or less to be empirically subjected to its procedures, and only then can we tell for certain whether or not the process will succeed. Add to this the fact of the relative rarity of psychoanalytic or psychotherapeutic practitioners and the exceedingly high cost of treatment, and an ambiguous situation arises which seems to betray its scientific paternity. The most that can be said with certainty about psychotherapy is that certain selected people in our culture who have nonphysical (or physically non-locatable) complaints; i.e., anxiety, guilt, obsession, compulsion, and organic-like complaints, seek interaction with a certain kind of (medical) person, and for which they pay by time, money, and energy. But we do not know why they and not their neighbors, who have similar difficulties, appear in the consulting room, and we do not know with any precision what troubles them in their deepest recesses.

Psychiatrists, psychologists, and social workers will formally acknowledge that they treat many people whom they do not consider diseased in a medical way.[5] The self-identified patient's discomfort is no less or no greater than thousands of their peers; but they seek either a complete freedom from the symptoms of pain, or a transcending ecstasy which comes temporarily from alcohol, drugs, sexual orgasm but which they then want more often than they have. They are often lonely, alienated, bored, frightened, or pained, but not to the level of social inhibition of the hysteric or depressive. But they can also at times reflect genuine neurotic symptoms or even ambulatory psychosis of all borderline varieties. They often represent the most gifted sections of the population, and they are invariably dissatisfied with the way their gifts and talents are being used. Are they sick? Should they be given psychotherapy? This depends upon a complex of factors and one's social vantage point; but we would say definitely that they are "existentially sick," and psychotherapy can help them. But if the therapist treats non-diseased people, then he is departing from the historical medical model of which he is an integral part, and severe tensions are thereby induced in him by this split. His ethical responsibility is to cure—and he charges a fee for it. But what if there is nothing to cure? There is simply the complaint of an existence no longer satisfying or tolerable for a number of reasons. How does one cure a fear of death, or a feeling of being a "hole," or of no purpose in life—particularly when religion, the usual reply to such queries, has more or less failed to be responsive in this area? This is not a frivolous thesis, for underneath the anxious or psychosomatic barrage the patient brings just such life questions are posed.

To better understand these matters we instituted a project involving doing psychotherapy with non-diseased subjects; the case reported here represents one such person treated. The criterion of non-disease for this study was that the subject had never before been treated by a psychiatrist, psychologist, or social worker in his lifetime, that he was functioning satisfactorily in personal, social, and occupational realms (by

---

[5] One psychiatrist of repute told us recently that half of his practice consists of non-diseased people. His referrals come from regular medical sources.

self-report and outside investigation), and that he came to psychotherapy at our request rather than through a felt need.[6]

Now on what theoretical or practical basis is such a subject justified? Here are a number of people going about their daily lives with more or less satisfaction. They then are offered the opportunity of spending twenty-five individual hours, for which they can see no good earthly reason, as a patient with a therapist.[7] They are oriented toward cooperation in scientific research, but to become a patient side by side with other paying patients is difficult for them to understand. Well, after some of their questions were satisfied, we simply said "If you have the time, why don't we just spend the twenty-five hours together and see what we discover about each other— what the fundamental ground of human relationships is— what our creative resources are." This and similar variations sufficed to enlist them, albeit with a context of some wit and anxiety.

In presenting the case history of Eric Swenson, a participant in this research, the possibly novel thesis will be proposed that the psychically diseased and the non-diseased are not polar opposites as we had formerly believed—that the lives of the diseased and non-diseased are fundamentally the same and differ only in their mode of being-in-the-world; that is, in the expression of their humanness. Both have the same problems of being man, feel despair in the same way, and both are thrown into the world without choice and leave it in the same way. The diseased and the non-diseased persons both seek an interpersonal integration based in love, and both employ the same coping mechanisms to find it. Possibly only the crucial intensity of existence in each differs from time to

---

[6] This procedure does not, of course, give us a "normal" or nondiseased sample. What it does do is provide subjects who have never used—and who have no immediate intention of using—psychotherapy as a means of problem-solving. They are nondiseased in the sense that they feel no need of such form of amelioration, take no steps to obtain it, and would not under any circumstances pay for it. They function without it. Possibly we would be on safer grounds here if we talked about "psychotherapeutically-involved and non-psychotherapeutically-involved" groups of people.

[7] A limit of twenty-five hours was set for each person in the experiment. This was arbitrary, but was all the time we had to give. In retrospection, this quantum served its function adequately.

148

time, and the historical and contemporaneous way in which the strain of the human condition is met.[8]

A clinician with a highly conventional orientation would be able to cite proof that Eric, the non-diseased patient reported on here, is indeed autistic, mildly paranoid, and possibly has a thinking disorder. But Pearce and Newton[9] see a paranoid integration as merely one of several developmental phases in *all* normal growth; some of society's most productive artists and others are autistic without being mentally ill as such;[10] and thinking disorders turn out to be no such thing once the inner world of the schizophrenic is penetrated and his message decoded. The point here is that autism, paranoid trends, and departures from logical thinking are socially pathological only when they are set within a framework of society's discontent with such departures. If they serve integration and creation, they cannot be judged socially pathological on any meaningful scale. And, of course, we have taken here the most extreme example of mental illness when, indeed, the most prevalent problems are the more subtle and innocuous-appearing phenomena.

People we call psychically non-diseased are more and more coming to psychoanalysis and psychoanalytic psychotherapy, not necessarily for the removal of their symptoms, but for the rediscovery of a lost creativity which gives a meaning and purpose to their existence. (They are of course also going to encounter groups, gestalt therapy, transactional analysis, etc.) They had id problems as in the past, but it is not the id which is disturbing the ego. It is the ego's relationship to the world—to people in it—and being-in-it as such, which

---

8 We may be accused here of either overlooking clinical facts or of imposing a metapsychological structure of some artificiality on such things as pain, suffering, and despair. To this one must say that it is demonstrated over and over again in treatment that pain, suffering and despair are reduced or disappear once the patient finds a creative or meaningful mode of existence. Clinical psychiatry suffers today from a concentration on the peripheral symptom and often misses the "heart" of the matter.

9 Pearce, J. and S. Newton. *The Conditions of Human Growth.* New York: Citadel Press, 1963.

10 Barron, F. *Creativity and Psychological Health.* New Jersey: D. Van Nostrand Company, 1962.

is the major problem. Psychotherapy deals with the subjective life and the impulses and behaviors which come from it. But so much of psychotherapy—designed to reduce repression—is itself repressive in format. Therapists fear their patients' impulses and acting-out, even their creativity, without understanding that inner and outer—subject and predicate —are an indissoluble unity. Deep hostile impulses and acting-out are to be feared only when they occur without a broader framework of existential meaning, that is, within a setting of nihilism. Control is not a problem if an impulse serves a higher creative aim—pleasure *qua* pleasure is emptiness; but pleasure in the form of an over-all and tight grand design is transcending. Thus by definition, therapy becomes the unfolding of the creative potential in the individual to the widest sense possible.

It seems probable that the psychoanalysis and psychoanalytic psychotherapy of the future will be reserved for already sufficiently creative people who want to reach even greater creative levels, or who want to recover a temporarily lost creativity. That is to say, that already expressive people will through therapy maximize their expressiveness, or extract the last iota from life itself. As it is, the majority of elective patients are intelligent, verbal, creative, and with strong achievement needs. They have a sense of guilt regarding a failure of self-actualization, and the Judaic and Protestant ethic drives them to produce as a source of self-worth. They everlastingly feel that they are missing the creative boat even if in reality they are not. This urge-to-creation and self-fulfillment in Western man is to be contrasted with the Oriental and African who has considerably less of such drives.

Just so long as such ethic operates in Western man, work and creation will be the basic source of his well-being, and therapy will need to stress this rather than "adjustment." Of course, creation here must not be interpreted as the production of a socially useful product but rather as the actualization of potential that gives an ontic sense of meaning and transcendence and unites one with his culture. It is the need to be-in-the-world as an unique part of the totality of humanness and to contribute to it. It may perhaps be that the

150

treatment of psychic illness will develop on several levels—this may already be the case today—and that the highest level will be the kind described here, whereas lower levels will involve instrumental and drug therapies of a quick nature and not called psychotherapy at all.

Patients who come to therapy are a selected group, and culture provides a pool of available people from which we make our choice.[11] But the nature of the pool is determined by social forces not yet delineated in any precise way. In every culture the healer has to fill a specific role; his limits are set by such role and are not easily modifiable. Today the hallmark of psychic healing is the "verbal symbol" and the therapeutic process becomes the vicissitudes of the symbol. We therapists have become adept at the use of such symbols, and we cater to culture's need for these liberating and transcending symbols. Symbolization and abstraction are thus both the curse and the salvation of Western man.

Whatever theoretical system is employed, the healing operations themselves often seem to come to the same thing.[12] We can only speculate as to the reasons for this. Some therapists, for example, Carl Rogers[13] and Marguerite Sechehaye,[14] place the emphasis on the "regard" of the therapist for his patient. Others consider the patient's "regard" for the therapist as critical. Still others stress the learning opportunities in treatment, or the emotional response to the special interaction of the two people. Any one of these views may be correct, or they all may be correct; we would modify the emphasis slightly by a simple generic addition to all of them. What determines the effectiveness of any psychotherapy is the depth of the encounter the therapy affords, its symbolic and ex-

---

11 We lack an exact definition of the psychotherapeutic patient. While we feel that we select the patients we treat, in fact they may be selecting us.

12 Ellis, A. Thoughts on theory versus outcome in psychotherapy. *Psychotherapy*, 1964, *1*, 83-87.

13 Rogers, C. R. *The interpersonal relationship: The core of guidance.* Harv. Educ. Rev., 1962, *32*, 416-429.

14 Sechehaye, M. *A New Psychotherapy in Schizophrenia.* New York: Grune & Stratton, 1956. *Symbolic Realization.* New York: International Univ. Press, 1951.

istential significance, and the opportunities it provides for Eros once again to function.[15]

People who come to therapy see themselves as symbolically dead and seek re-creation. Many reveal that they "feel dead in life." The id and the superego then have to be seen within this larger framework, and the pleasure principle becomes over-limiting as an explanatory principle, particularly for the mature individual. Psychotherapy is the joint discovery of re-creativity—that it is still present under the facade of symptoms—that it transcends the symptoms—that it provides a motive force for a newer existence. Psychotherapy today in its quest for scientific discipline limits its treatment goals at the same time it artistically approaches its subject. It then perforce must deny a part of the data which the encounter produces since its artistic approach does not permit quantification or replication. In this behavioral modificaton comes off better but suffers in still another way.

PROLOGOMENON TO PSYCHOTHERAPY

Eric Swenson is a twenty-year-old senior psychology major at a large and important Western university. He is blond, on the tall side, wears a crew-cut, and is not remarkably different from the average fraternity member in his university. His speech is crisp but clear, and he avoids intellectualisms or affectations. He is almost the all-American prototype of the middle-class stereotype.

Eric has a slight sense of unease about him. He seems to be searching, but this is not an overt anxiety. It is rather like finding one's place under changing circumstances. He was selected for treatment from seven other candidates because he not only met the criterion of psychic non-disease given above, but because his disinterest and even hostility toward psychotherapy challenged us. He agreed to come regularly for the twenty-five hours, but he did not necessarily agree to participate in the relationship. Obviously, as is also true in

---

[15] Eros has in modern times become corrupted to mean principally sexuality, which is itself a sign of the dehumanization of our times. We are here returning it to its original Greek and broader usage.

the patients we accept for a fee, he attracted us by his obvious intelligence, his upper-middle-class social background, his verbal facility and desire to learn, and by the fact that he represented modern-day university youth.[1] (He attended the same university from which we had received a Ph.D. some twenty years earlier.) Eric denied having any problems or ever having sought counseling or psychotherapeutic help. He said he was happy at home, was making good grades, was a senior leader in his fraternity, and pointed to a host of similar achievements. Of course, while all of this was true, it later turned out that he had dissatisfactions in several areas. Probably the tone of his mode-of-being at the time is best given by the following dream which came later and which will be left largely uninterpreted in the Freudian sense.

I was tied upside down from the ceiling of a hall, helpless. Someone pushing me, making me swing, then laughing about the control which he was exercising over me. It seemed that it was not he who tied me, but some large organization. The next thing I knew, this man was also tied, but not upside down.

I found that I could wriggle free from my bonds, and was soon free. My first response was to somehow tease the man (who was still tied), or otherwise show him that now *I* had the upper hand. Instead, I untied him. I was glad, because now we were both together in our illegal attempt to escape from the "organization." As we hopefully crouched on the floor, about to plan our escape, I saw two large shadows on the floor in front of us. My heart sank. I turned around to see two men in uniforms, smiling. They had known all the time that I never had a chance.

Eric in his dream presents the existential problem of unfreedom—of constriction—of communality and divorcement —of despair and suspiciousness—of the odds against him in an organized world. He also reveals the "becoming possibilities" inherent in his "lack of freedom," and the fact that he seeks desperately to actualize his being.

---

[1] This was written more than a decade ago and may not be so true today.

The Swenson family is a large one. In addition to Eric there are five siblings, ages nineteen, sixteen, eleven, eight and six years of age. Four are boys and two are girls. Eric, of course, is the oldest. A good family life is an important ideal to the Swensons, and nothing is permitted to stand in the way of it. There is a family discipline which reminds one of the Puritans who settled this Country, or the Quakers or Amish. Personal feeling is probably sacrificed for the group good, and arbitrary individual action of an hysterical kind would be severely frowned upon. While Eric has most in common with Frank, his brother next in age, there is no deep sharing of experience or feeling as can occur between brothers.

Now, because Eric represents a non-diseased person, and because it may be difficult to grasp why he should even stay in therapy for twenty-five hours, the following excerpt from a tape recording which came at about the twelfth hour gives us something about the way he conceives of himself and his attitudes.

> *Dr. B.:* Eric, would you say that your problem is one of a gap between practice and an ideal rather than a neurotic situation? If you were willing to settle for less then there would be no problem?
>
> *Eric:* Right.
>
> *Dr. B.:* Well, what do you think about this business?
>
> *Eric:* Well, really, you see, I don't know that much about what constitutes a neurotic—I haven't ever thought of myself that way.
>
> *Dr. B.:* You haven't.
>
> *Eric:* Well, this has always been what I thought has been my problem—that I do have an ideal—that I do look at my capabilities and say, "Well, I can do this," and yet I don't do it. And I do see, you know, I would like to—even with girls—I figure, well, heck, you know they're really going to like me because of the kind of guy I am, and yet I'm still kind of afraid with them. Sure, I'd like to be a great lover.

154

You know, I was thinking of something else today that, well, I don't really want to be a conformist. The fact that I used to smoke Pall Malls—and everybody smokes Pall Malls, so I changed to Philip Morris. Then I tried these Old Golds which I don't like, just so I could be smoking something different from somebody else. I like the idea that I'm smarter than other people, that I can think things out for myself where they can't, that I can come to a better decision than they can, and yet, I don't allow myself to use this ability in a self-situation. I'll just retreat or give a kind of all-knowing glance, you know, like "Well, I know what's going on here," but I'm not going to fight it—there's nothing I can do about it but go ahead and act stupid.

Dr. B.: H'mm.

Eric: I was wholly avoiding your question. But I'm not in a constant state of—how I conceive a neurotic is in a constant state of agitation about everything— because when I do think things out of a hole, that's the kind of hole it is—where I realize that I'm different from these guys. I have different ideas, and yet, I'll let them go on as they are. Even though I don't feel this is right, that's what I do because I don't want to get hurt. So, I just let it go and I don't feel terribly bad about it all the time, but there are times when I do. And I can go along for months just perfectly happy in my little cubbyhole, but the more I'm in this the more I realize that it is a cubbyhole. I'm kind of, as you can see, wrapped up in this cyclical kind of thinking. Do you have any thoughts from an outsider that might lend something to the situation? Do you think I'm neurotic?

Dr. B.: I'm indifferent to that question. I do think you have a discrepancy between your functioning and your ideals—that some people ignore it, or can ignore it, and others can't or don't want to.

Eric: I've always had hope for myself. I've always considered that I'll do well. I always when I go into a test I figure that I'll get an A on it. I consider that I

155

will do well in my life work—I figure that I will get a girl that is right for me—that has all the qualities that I like. I see these things in the future, and yet I'm getting more and more disgusted with evidence coming through that I'm not doing anything now to help myself toward that.

Dr. B.: Do you sometimes feel like it is a problem at all?

Eric: Not if I think about it. A lot of times I don't think about it. If I think about it, I'll realize that there is a problem.

Dr. B.:. Well, why don't you make the decision, then, to live a more authentic life?

Eric: Because I have things—some of them which have been brought out here—they are my needs, they are irrational, they are the cause of fears but they are still there, and maybe if I could bring them out I could see them, maybe I can do something about them. Maybe I can't. Maybe they will just prey on my mind all the more. Or maybe I'll give in to them more and more when I realize what they are.

Dr. B.: You feel that it isn't in your power to be more authentic because of these irrationalities?

Eric: Well, I certainly have—somewhere there is a desire to be more authentic. I don't know if it is in my power or not, and I don't even know what authentic is, yet. And I don't completely give in. I'll often retreat instead of fighting a battle that I don't feel is good, that would do any good. I couldn't convince those guys to be any different during Hell Week. I've worked on them a little bit—guys that I feel could understand. I kind of slip my views in, you know. But I'm not going to face up to them—I'm not going to make them my enemies. And sometimes—you're right—sometimes I don't give a damn! Just too much effort—is what I feel most of the time. But then when I come to the point—sometimes I come to the point and it just depresses me when I see the way that things are, and I feel that I

156

should exert the effort but I don't. Whether it is in my power or not, I don't know. Whether it would be advantageous or not—I don't know. Whether I would lead a richer life. You see, I'm still looking for the things like sex and drinking and being one of the boys, that I didn't really have until I got in college, that I missed, you know, and I wanted to try it. And now that I'm starting to, you know, try these things. You know, I read a little more and get a little more sophisticated and they become less important to me and I have to start looking further ahead, which doesn't answer the question in your mind. I'll have to start answering pretty soon as far as my profession goes, I suppose.

As the therapeutic hours proceeded Eric became more and more like our paying patients, so that we tended to forget that he was not present for help. He developed a classical transference, and we a classical countertransference. We had difficulty recalling that he was merely part of an experiment and that we were to remain empirically dispassionate and objective. Interestingly enough, the necessary tension and substrate anxiety which motors all psychotherapy was present in sufficient quantity even though no disabling neurotic symptom as such was present in quantity as the focus of the encounter.[16] The encounter progression was basically carried, not only by what we came to be represented to him by the past—transference—but a contemporaneous meeting in the present with all of its being-with possibilities. There was a subtle therapeutic reinforcement in each other of the creative properties of *discovery, integration,* and *application,* as occurs in any act of original creation. This was both binding and liberating for us, and no formal analysis of the transference was ever required to attain the therapeutic outcomes reported later.

If Eric had a problem in the therapeutic sense, it was that he sought greater self-actualization and authenticity as a per-

---

[16] Based upon our experience with Eric and others like him, we now feel that the requirement of a neurotic symptom for progression in psychotherapy is partly mythical.

157

son. He had a number of personality defenses which permitted him to take a lofty view of himself and his world, and such a view deprived him of fruition. But he had not consciously realized this when he came to the experiment, and one wonders if, and when, he might have without our intervention. Eric could have established a fully average, defensible adult life as he was going, and have taken in stride incompleteness, ennui, indifference, moderate attainment, pleasure, and a marriage based on convention, etc. But both Eric and society would have been shortchanged by such a life.

PROBLEM THEMAS

Put more formally, the problem themas of Eric's existence were as follows:

1. *Being-With.* Most relevant to Eric's existence were his interpersonal difficulties. We had the opportunity of observing him in social situations—the hospital where he trained for a summer—and would rate him above average in interpersonal relationships for his peer group, but his feelings were that he could never penetrate to the heart of his respondent. He felt that he invariably missed the target by an infinitesimal amount; but miss it he did. This subtle difficulty seemed real as we perceived it. Missing the mark then led to a whole host of fine concealing mechanisms designed to protect him from the realization of his basic alienation. (Such alienation in Eric cannot be called schizoid in any sense of the word, either in terms of the Rorschach Test or the Minnesota Multiphasic Personality Inventory which a colleague gave him, or by clinical observations made of him.) These mechanisms ranged from an overweening interest in poker—to the disadvantage of academic matters—to Don Juanism, or to a self-righteousness which directly countered his weakness. But there were also more subjective and subtle mechanisms involving self-worth. He wanted to be fair, honest, and open —but *so* fair, honest, and open that it was itself the reflection of a closed system.

It was only with mother that he lost this sense of unease; but this was counterpoised by a displaced alienation from his father who, in a sense, paid for the mother-son relationship. As he grew older, even mother failed as the source of deepest comfort, possibly because of a growing self-consciousness on the part of each of the sexual implications of their relationship.

His father was an avid churchgoer, a fundamentalist from the Midwest, who by perseverance and grit had reached the level of principal of a large high school. He was respected in every way by both his students and his faculty. At the time of writing this report, he had attained some notice by sending a girl student home because he considered her coiffure outlandish for high school, and even though her mother threatened to sue the board of education, he did not back off. He tended to run his home in the same way he did his school, and Eric often had difficulty seeing the man behind the principal. In hour after hour he reiterated how "fair" his father was. Only in the arena of money could Eric feel that his father was not always the Mosaic figure he appeared to him.

We interviewed Mr. Swenson (with Eric) toward the end of the treatment and found him a well-meaning person, but so insensitive to his son's needs that he was genuinely astonished at the visible tension between them. He couldn't at all understand that his son might be alienated from him. He gropingly tried to cope with this revelation in a highly intellectual fashion, but not necessarily with a hostile defensiveness of any sort. It was rather that he expected a father-son relationship to fall into the ancient and honorable pattern established by his forebears, in which the roles were more or less fixed and emotion played little part. He did not behave as though his son was his rival, and he would have laughed at the idea that there was competition for his wife in the Oedipal sense.

2. *Being-in-the-Hole.* Eric attracts many girls, but he classifies them along two parameters: "pigs" and "good" girls. The former are simply to sleep with on a one- or two-shot deal; the latter cannot be touched in any way. Even so, denigrating the first group—all of whom are also "good" girls by con-

ventional standards—does not leave him comfortable, for be-ing-in-the-hole with a "good" girl makes him guilty, if he does not supply what he thinks is the proper affection or "giving" to go with it. And this he cannot often do. He also tends to see sexuality as aggressing-against and the recipient as a help-less victim. He ardently woos the good girls but drops them when being-in-the-hole is expected of him. He unconsciously develops disaffections with the girl which eventually termi-nate the relationship. But he is not satisfied to go on without equality, which many of them would be willing to do. Eric feels that to do so would deny both partners a mature growth, and an improper marriage might result.

Conventionally, it would appear that Eric has a castration complex, and it would be possible to make formulations about his situation in this way. However, Eric is not *actually* castrated, and he does not behave like a castrate. He is potent, has no masturbation defenses, and rather seeks a total rela-tionship with a woman which involves being-in-the-hole as well as feeling a transcending tenderness for her. He thus has his total growth with a woman in mind rather than merely a physiological experience.

Eric knew that this kind of classificatory behavior of women was arbitrary and left him with considerable guilt after a relationship experience with both types of girls. He also felt guilty about his complicity in making them fall in love with him and then dropping them. Eric was attracted by beauty, and while he verbalized that it was skin-deep, he could not reduce its comparative pull among all of the virtues which were really more important to him.

3. Being-in-Love. Being-in-love is one form of being-with, and possibly its most intense manifestation. It deserves sep-arate treatment here because all forms of being relate to this one.

Eric has trouble being-in-the-hole because he has trouble being-in-love. Since he cannot get to the heart of the girl he considers a marital candidate, he cannot bring the proper affection to being-in-the-hole. Now for most boys, this would be of little consequence, but it looms large for Eric, for this is the way he is. While his fraternity pressures him to conform to manhood by getting notches "on his gun," he holds out for a transcending love which he is certain exists but which he cannot yet define or find. So at times he bends with the pressure of the fraternity and at other times stays aloof from it. But he wants very desperately to love and to be loved, and is now beginning to understand that love is an interpersonal attitude and experience which reaches into all relationships as the building blocks of existence. He feels guilty and ecstatic about the possibilities of love and understands that it is the leaven and the cement of all deep and fundamental human relationships. But the ego pulls back at surrender and is then urged forward by the id. Someone, he feels, gets cheated in marriage; and in this case he unconsciously believes it is the woman; his mother. But why is love reductive rather than ennobling? Could it be that in the Swenson family there was always the form but not the spirit of creative love—that someone always felt emotionally cheated, not necessarily by deprivation but by the significant absence of integrated tenderness? It is normal under such circumstances for a boy to feel that the woman, the mother, gets the brunt of such deficiency which the father either withholds or offers. Can it be that Eric's guilt in regard to the emotional dryness of his family is the barrier to his complete participation with woman, and also accounts for the angry feelings toward his father?

Interpersonal therapy tends to see the ability to love and be tender as the central problem of interpersonal relationships. No true fulfillment is possible without deep and meaningful tenderness, for this provides the meaning-structure upon which other events are projected. In psychotherapy, the most flagrant and insidious of symptoms often drop away when love and tenderness become possible for the patient. But the important point is that tenderness and creativity are intimately related, and one grows out of the other. Eros is in this sense also the source of creativity, and this is what therapy makes possible in a corrective way. Anxiety is the absence of love. Eric's family anxiety is a part of his existential anxiety—his place in the world—and his guilt is the

161

existential guilt of not living up to his ideals and expectations. Thus, to understand Eric and ameliorate his condition it does not necessarily help to invoke concepts of neurotic anxiety or neurotic guilt in the classical Freudian sense.

4. *Being-in-Time-and-Space.* Eric's being is compressed in space—he feels the need and plans to travel soon for a year—and temporality is his onus. He calculates time rather than lives it. Acts are valued against other acts in terms of the time they take. Time replaces money as the existential symbolic binder. People who accept their finiteness, or who successfully masquerade an infiniteness, do not fall into Eric's state. Thus, the world shrinks and dilates as the psychological meaning of his time and space fluctuate—and they tend to fluctuate with the state of his feelings of tenderness. The systems open and provide freedom *to be* and to progress when he feels tender. When he does not, space and time close in to narrow his world. When his world becomes extremely narrow, then the fear of death or mental illness supervenes.

THE COURSE OF PSYCHOTHERAPY

The foregoing observations were all derived from the ongoingness of the therapy itself, and it only remains to describe something of its course and its outcomes. As previously stated, Eric was conceptualized and treated side by side with patients—and as though he were a patient who had applied for help. We did not charge him a fee only because he had no funds of his own and we did not want a fee to come from his father; otherwise, the conditions of treatment were the same.

The initial status of psychotherapy varied somewhat from the usual patient. The latter usually comes loaded with anxiety and a set of complaints, and one usually waits passively until the facade is drained. Eric came without this, so more of a dialogue was consequently indicated. He used the first hour gingerly to make clear that he had no problem and was not a patient. Indeed, we sympathized with him for neither

162

of us knew exactly how to proceed with each other.* We re-inforced the nature of the experiment, and restated that two people with professional intent to be systematically together could discover a great deal about themselves in terms of their growth—that he might be willing to try it. Since he was training to become a psychologist, he wanted a professional identification with us, but he did not permit this to interfere with the acceptance of a patient status. The end of the first hour left us both uncertain, but he agreed to return and actually kept every single one of his twenty-five appointments. As a matter of fact, when it was necessary for us to cancel two appointments he eagerly asked for make-up times.

At the end of the third hour he had worked through the uniqueness of being a "patient without an illness" and could see that the relationship might help with certain existential and personality questions he had had and from time to time posed to himself in unguarded moments. All of the usual manifestations of the transference then slowly became evident. This appeared particularly when he began verbalizing about his father whom he likened to me in various respects. His position vis-á-vis his father was an ambiguous one: he both revered and hated him. He admired his scholarship, administrative ability, and his voluntary church work, but saw him deficient in warmth, insight, and comradeliness. It later turned out that some of these weaknesses he also attributed to me.

From his father, he could go on to talk about his mother and tell me of certain historical situations in his growth which he felt had dependent, pleasurable, or sexual overtones. We mentioned the word Oedipus to him, knowing full well that no clinical psychologist in training could escape that unfortunate Theban. He overreacted with much hostility to this, but it seemed more mother-directed than father-directed. He said that he could understand an attachment between a male child and a mother but severely rejected the Freudian formulation of this particular event (which may thereby in itself give it credence!) .

---

* He was the first non-diseased person we treated in this research.

163

In the middle third of treatment he was able to bring up the problems of being-with, being-in-love, and being-in-the-hole. He recognized his need, not necessarily to achieve, but to come to fulfillment—to be authentic—and verbalized that regardless of attainments, he would never reach his goals if his interpersonal relationships were not changed. For the first time he could see his defensive mode-of-being, and that, on one count or another, he had been fencing with people. He was particularly distressed at his dichotomization of women, and it genuinely hurt him to denigrate any woman. He intellectually knew that there are no good and bad women—just women who become what they are because of their own existence. This sexual attitude mirrored a phobia toward life in its positiveness and had to be seen in this framework rather than as a simple competition device in his family. Nor did we see any basis for postulating anything homosexual which could help us.

In the final third of the hours he developed an intense hostility toward us which we only incompletely resolved by the end of the twenty-five hours. But we interpreted the total resistance of his being to the deeper insights and understanding of his life. We also conventionally interpreted the transference in terms of his historical father and mother, but this took a back seat to his total creative setting as a person. He then made attempts to bring his mode-of-being more in line with his new-found insights. He began to merge the bad and good girls—and to see them more as people than as holes or as goddesses. He let them get closer and feel him. He stopped being shattered by occasional rejections of his invitations to them, and he began to enjoy being-with-them for its own sake. He now played poker in the fraternity for its social-gain quality rather than an all-consuming defense against studying and interacting with people. His grades improved and as a graduating senior he began thinking of delaying entrance into graduate school while he spent a year away from his parents in the world of work, possibly in Europe.

Because twenty-five hours of therapy were arbitrarily set as the empirical quantum of treatment and did not necessarily fit the needs of any single patient, we asked him to write to us if he felt the need for it, and told him that we would arrange for infrequent interviews as a follow-up. In the five months since termination he has not used the written document form of communication, but he did call us for an interview. This interview took place about two months before this was written.

He has preserved and extended his gains in all areas. Eric is by self-report and observation much more of a person, happier, and much readier to help people as a future psychologist and man. Not that Eric has overcome all his felt deficiencies. He still has some trouble with girls. It is rather that he now understands that these are existential deficiencies and knows how to go about altering them. He has made the choice to be authentic, but it will require years of living before we really know how effective our work was.

CONCLUSION

This unconventional case history is offered here for heuristic purposes only to illustrate the unity of the personalities of the diseased and non-diseased. Most of us secretly believe that the neurotic and psychotic are a different order of people, and that separate theoretical and meliorative systems of human change apply. Working with Eric Swenson, and others, as though they were patients, has convinced us that what distinguishes the patient from the non-patient is something entirely different from what we had formerly supposed. Becoming-a-patient is sometimes a selective fact of culture, or of opportunity, or of social coercion. It is not analogous to the person who has a fever and for whom a microbe or other infectious organ is demonstrable. Psychic illness, in many aspects, seems to be a disorder of the patterning or integration of existence and its meaning rather than a disease as such. It is gauged by the state of Eros and Thanatos rather than by a thermometer—the life and death forces which are at the basis of creativity. In this sense we are all diseased and all non-diseased. We suffer from humanity and the human condition.

Such thesis is more than mere philosophizing, for it has the greatest of implications for the treatment of men. If therapy restores wholeness, purpose, and creativity to the patient, and if this should turn out to be its prime mode of viability, should we not stop trying to find mental disease on the basis of the ancient medical analogue? Should we not give greater thought to the basic nature of creativity, and to the social possibilities of creativity and meaning for more people than even therapy makes possible? Is it not, then, the particularly gifted who will receive the psychoanalysis and psychoanalytic therapy of the future, since in the face of the rising demand and fewer therapists our selection is becoming narrower and narrower? Most of us are already treating large numbers of non-diseased patients if we look carefully at our practice. Is it fantasy to believe this could eventually rise for some of us to close to 100%?

The case of Eric Swenson makes it possible for us to integrate to some extent the disintegrating theoretical findings of psychotherapy. It reveals that classification of disease and non-disease in personality are often arbitrary acts of the observer because we conceptualize them along this parameter to begin with as a professional bias. Beneath the divergencies of therapeutic theory lies the core concept of existence as creation and re-creation in a complex and myriad of forms. When this dynamic re-creation ceases, death—or its symbolic equivalent, psychic illness—supervenes.

Other researchers seem to be coming independently to a similar point of view. Maslow[17] says in a recent paper "My feeling is that the concept of creativeness and the concept of the healthy, self-actualizing, fully-human person seems to be coming closer and closer together, and may perhaps turn out to be the same thing." Carl Rogers in his recent formulations comes very close to saying the same.

[17] Maslow, A. H. The creative attitude. *The Structurist*, 1963, No. 3, pp. 4-10.

CHAPTER XIII

Conclusions

THE HUMAN EQUATION is ever present in the psychotherapeutic process whether a cognitive treatment is involved or a more humanistic one. What cures seems to be the presence of someone professional who cares, who listens, and who has the deepest empathy for the patient—in an old culture which no longer cares or listens. The curative aspect of treatment lies in the interpersonal mysterium of the participants, which then becomes incorporated into the intrapsychic level, and finally leads to motor change. People have effects on each other; intimate people have intimate effects.

Therapy essentially deals with the mental representations of significant historical people and recasts them into a *now* or *present* mode, and these representations, if deep and significant, come forth as a new existential gestalt, a new meaning to old compulsive behaviors. Psychotherapy is basically a matter of archetypes, the universal forces which have governed every person and every culture since the first two people were on earth. Such archetypes transform psychic energy and are endowed with potential for growth. It does not matter what

167

a therapeutic system calls them for they are nevertheless present and operative in every treatment.

Sexuality is no longer the reason for coming to a psychoanalysis or a psychotherapy. Freud's formulation of repressed pleasure wishes as the basic neurotic conflict no longer applies in the final reaches of the 20th Century. Where a sexual problem is indeed in the central focus of the psyche, "practical" clinics of the Masters-Johnson type teach one "how to do it," or one perhaps joins a commune. But this does not mean that patients do not bring sexual problems to psychotherapy. Quite the contrary. It does mean that the deeper reasons for coming to this form of process are rather ego, social, and existential than id or instinctual. Any therapist who fails to recognize this is still practicing in the time of Sigmund Freud.

Psychotherapists have been at once over-modest and over-arrogant about their contribution to society. They need to be more self-convinced about their work and mission, and need to present a new and revised image of psychotherapy to society. The greatest attack on it has come not from the outside but from within—from unregenerated psychotherapists who became unconvinced about themselves and the work they were doing day after day.

The profession of psychotherapy is a satisfying career set in a dissatisfying prenumbra. That is, the analytic process itself does not *let-be,* so that a certain turbulence is always present in our work. The analogy might be made to an aircraft which is always in slightly bumpy air. But that is the way all family relationships are, and life itself, as well. How could it be different? Therapy is having a skilled pilot to transcend the cliffs of Scylla and Charybdis.

The concluding message of this book is a simple one: that the psychotherapist has an obligation and responsibility to his own experiencing and growth and must recognize his formal training as only a mere beginning. With such a philosophy of growth, his therapeutic hours become living ones and, because of this, conducive to bringing tremendous change to the lives of his patients.

ACKNOWLEDGMENT

"The Adoration of the Patient and Its Disillusionment,"
"Therapist Satisfaction," "The Therapist as Patient," and
"The Fully Analyzed Patient" first appeared in a different
version in the *American Journal of Psychoanalysis*. "Hope
and Psychotherapy" was first published in a varying form in
the *Psychoanalytic Review*. "The Presentation of the Face in
Psychotherapy" was released in the journal *Psychotherapy;*
the "Interminable Patient" showed in *Voices*. "The Therapy
of a Non-Diseased Person" was a part of my symposium,
Modern Psychotherapeutic Practice. Permission to use this
material has been granted.

Index

Abraham, P. 126
Adler, A. 10, 11, 15, 17, 18
Adler, K. A. 10
Aesculapius 41
Agape 106
Alcoholics Anonymous 93
Anxiety, as absence of love 161
Archetypes 14, 16, 19, 86, 167
Aristotle 3

"Bad" parent 62
Barron, F. 149
Bartenders, as therapists 99, 110-112
Beckett, S. 120, 122
Behavioral modification therapy 51, 85, 152
Benny, Jack 138
Berle, Milton 138
Berne, E. 15
Beyond transference 19
Bioenergetics 51
Birdwhistell, R. L. 126
Bleuler, M. 141
"Book of the It" 21
Bosch, H. 104
Bowlby, J. 134
Buddha 3
Bugental, J. 112
Burton, A. 5, 8, 11, 14, 18, 20, 28, 30, 32, 35, 37, 42, 45, 61, 67, 92, 93, 94, 98, 142

Camus, A. 116
"Central Purpose" (Adler) 11
Charcot, J. M. 21, 83
Client-centered counseling 20, 85, 117
Collective unconscious 14
Copernicus 25
Countertransference 18, 43 ,

Darwin, C. 15, 25
Daytop 93
Dialogue of Self and Other 4
Don Quixote 23
Dostoevski, F. 35

Ego 13
Ego, as provider of hope 135
Einstein, A. 15
El Greco 130
Ellis, A. 30, 32, 34, 53, 58, 90, 151
Encounter group 9, 19, 44, 51, 56, 85
End-point goals in psychotherapy 98
English, O. S. 30, 32, 33, 34, 35
Erikson, E. H. 134
Eris 12, 43
Eros 12, 42, 43, 64, 106, 137, 138, 165
Esalen Foundation 66
Existentialism 67 ,
Existential neurosis 13, 103
Expectancy neurosis 122-123

Faith dynamics 85
Faith dynamics, disturbance of 80

171

Family romance 42, 87
Farson, R. 52
Fate analysis theories 128
Faulkner, W. 115
Fine, R. 30
Fitzgerald, F. Scott 19, 35
Fox, R. 32
Frank, J. D. 134,
Frankl, V. 141
Freud, S. 3, 9, 10, 13, 14, 15, 16, 17, 18,
    20, 21, 22, 23, 25, 26, 29, 31, 33, 35,
    39, 40, 41, 42, 43, 47, 48, 53, 54, 70,
    81, 83, 86, 88, 94, 102, 105, 108, 110,
    117, 118, 122, 126, 126, 141, 168
Fromm-Reichmann, F. 61, 73, 142
Fully functioning person 56, 102

Galen 106
Ghandi, M. 68
Godot Complex 120, 121, 123
Goffman, E. 27, 127, 132, 144
Goya 104, 130
Groddek, G. 20-21

Hegel, G. W. F. 3
Heidegger, M. 38, 67
Helen of Troy 121
Henry, W. E. 11, 69, 74
Hesse, H. 7, 17, 115
Hillman, J. 18
Hippocrates 41
Horney, K. 56
Hope:
    as energizer 137
    bridge between reality and fantasy
        137
    as biological influence 138
    and laughter 138
    and temporality 138-139
    time as enemy of 139
    freedom-in-time, as help for 139
    in manic-depressives 139
    in schizophrenics 139-140
    loss of 140
Hope, Bob 138
Human condition 15, 65, 67, 83, 100,
    135
Huxley, A. 108
Hypnotherapy 51

Inferiority and power theory 17
Interminable psychotherapy:
    Motivation, basis for 114-118, 119
    Administrative solutions for 118-119

Janik, A. 25
Jessel, G. 138
Jung, C. G. 12, 13, 14, 15, 17, 20, 22,
    39, 43, 54, 57, 66, 70, 71, 81, 83,
    102, 110, 141

Kasanin, J. S. 141
Kazantzakis, N. 115
Kierkegaard, S. 67
Koop, S. 12
Kretschmer, W. 57
Krisnamurti 3
Kuhn, T. S. 22, 25

Laing, R. 12, 66
Lao-tse 3,
Lavoisier, A. L. 25
Life Style:
    adaptations from the introject 14
    as basis of therapeutic style 16
    definitions 12-13
    personal, of the healer 10, 19, 20
    personality pattern 10
Lopez-Ibor, J. J. 14
Lowen, A. 131
LSD 5, 66
Luce, Henry 19

Maimonides 106
Marijuana 66
Marx, K. 3
Maslow, A. H. 112, 145, 166
Masters-Johnson 168
Meditation 56
Melges, F. T. 134
Mendel, W. 14, 30, 36
Mesmer, F. 10
Miller, H. 35
Mosak, L. 12
Moses 47
Mowrer, O. H. 133

Newton, I. 25
Newton, S. 149
Nietzsche, F. 17

Oedipus 163
Ontogenetic thrust 73
Other 56, 57, 86

Pavlov, I. P. 5
Pearce, J. 149
Perls, F. 24, 88

Pfister, O. 16
Plato 3
Polster, E. 32, 24
Primal scream therapy 10, 23, 51
Psilocybine 5
Psychodrama 44, 51
Psychotherapists of schizophrenia:
    characteristics of 72-74
    Motivation, questionnaire and re-
    sponses 63-65, 68-76
    Vocational choice 60-61
Psychotherapy:
    Basic definition 4
    End-point goals in 98-110
    Intensive relationships of 42

Radical psychiatry 9, 55
Rank, O. 15, 53
Rational-emotive therapy 85
Reich, W. 15, 22
Resistance 16, 79, 98
    cultural, to change 23
Rieff, P. 67
Rilke, R. M. 109
Roazen, P. 53
Rogers, C. R. 5, 13, 20, 21, 30, 34, 38,
    52, 53, 54, 55, 80, 102, 117, 145,
    151, 166
Rosen, J. 53, 58

Schizophrenia:
    as life style 14
    as primary form of existence 62
    as "walking death" 64
    characteristics of 66-68
    treatment of chronic 18, 20
Schizophrenics:
    "at liberty" 14
    soul, riddle of the 18

Schwing, G. 73
Searles, H. 60
Sechehaye, M. 73, 142, 151
Self realization 102, 104, 109
Sheldon, W. 57
Socarides, C. W. 140
Spranger, O. 57
Steinzor, B. 30, 32, 35, 45
Suicide 16, 48, 62, 90
Sullivan, H. S. 61, 63
Synanon 93
Synchronicity 16, 22
Szasz, T. 20, 116, 144
Szondi, L. 128
Szondi Test 128

Thanatos 12, 42, 64, 68, 90, 106, 137,
    138, 165
Thorne, F. 58
Tiepolo, G. B. 104
Touching the body 16
Toulmin, S. 25
Transactional analysis 9, 10, 44, 51
Transference 16, 18, 19, 83

Von Domarus, E. 141

Warkentin, J. 30, 34, 35
Watson, J. D. 137
Wheelis, A. 9
Will, O. A., Jr. 61
Will therapy 53
"Wise Old Man" (Jung) 83, 141
Wittgenstein, L. 9, 18

Zweig, A. 16